P9-CDD-511

Paul Horgan

Twayne's United States Authors Series

Kenneth Eble, Editor

University of Utah

TUSAS 459

PAUL HORGAN
c. 1979
Photograph by William Van Saun, Wesleyan University

Paul Horgan

By Robert Gish

University of Northern Iowa

Twayne Publishers • Boston

Paul Horgan

Robert Gish

Published by Twayne Publishers
A Division of G. K. Hall & Company
70 Lincoln Street
Boston, Massachusetts 02111

Book Production by Marne B. Sultz

Book Design by Barbara Anderson

Printed on permanent/durable acid-free paper and bound in the United States of America.

Library of Congress Cataloging in Publication Data

Gish, Robert.
Paul Horgan.

(Twayne's United States authors series; TUSAS 459)
Bibliography: p. 135
Includes index.
1. Horgan, Paul, 1903– —Criticism and interpretation. I. Title. II. Series.
PS3515.06583Z66 1983 813'.52 83–12611
ISBN 0–8057–7399–1

For Judy and Robin,
Annabeth and Tim

Contents

About the Author

Robert Gish was born in Albuquerque, New Mexico, in 1940. He attended the Albuquerque public schools, New Mexico State University, and the University of New Mexico from which he earned his undergraduate and graduate degrees. For several years he taught at Valley High School in Albuquerque, moving in 1967 to the University of Northern Iowa where he is presently professor of English language and literature. He received an NDEA graduate fellowship to study at California State University, Fullerton, and an NEH postdoctoral fellowship for study at the University of California, Davis. He is the author of several scholarly articles and monographs ranging in subject from Bloomsbury to the American West. He is a regular contributing reviewer to the *North American Review* and to several Midwest dailies. His professional memberships include the Rio Grande Writers Association and the Western Literature Association.

Preface

It is one of life's ironies that I did not read anything by Paul Horgan until I moved to Iowa—from New Mexico, the setting for a large number of his books. Throughout the "land of enchantment," Horgan is regarded as a native son, not merely because of his many books about New Mexico, but because he grew up in Albuquerque, lived in Roswell and Santa Fe, and—since moving to Connecticut—returns for visits at least once each year.

I too grew up in Albuquerque. And, as I was to find out, I attended the same high school Horgan attended some forty years before me. Moreover, I stayed several days as a Boys Stater at New Mexico Military Institute where Horgan was once enrolled as a cadet and subsequently worked as librarian. Ironic. Finding Horgan as I did, in "exile" (a prominent theme in his life and work), has meant more to me than had I read him when I lived in New Mexico. What Horgan has helped me realize is that somehow the West is in all of us and is a very major part of whatever the American experience is.

All of which is another way of saying that even though Horgan is often considered a "regionalist," he isn't. At least he is not a regionalist in any lesser, pejorative way. Another irony. Coming from the East to the West as he did, and then returning to the East, his perspective spans the entire country—and then some. So the irony of discovering his writing while living in Iowa has been a fortunate paradox. It has allowed me a middle distance, a pivotal place from which to look out—to the East and to the West—and appreciate the transcontinental perspective of Horgan, one of our honored but somewhat neglected American authors.

The scope of this study of Horgan's life and writing is broad and, because it is introductory by nature, necessarily brief. Horgan has lived a long and productive life and I try to show that it is of a whole, his biography affecting his art, his versatility as a man of letters, his talent and ability as a painter and a "musician" all merging by means of "analogous form" with his values as a Yankee plainsman and Christian humanist.

I have attempted in the ordering of my discussion to illustrate how human character is of fundamental importance throughout his essays, short fiction, novels, histories, and biographies. Thus I argue, light-handedly I hope, that Horgan is essentially a biographer—a portraitist of persons, and happenings. My arrangement and assumptions are not so much chronological as they are regional and generic. In addition to maybe making his writings more accessible to readers, my hope is that I might generate more serious scholarly consideration of an important American writer.

Robert Gish

University of Northern Iowa

Acknowledgments

There are many people who have helped me in the preparation of this book and to whom I am grateful. I wish to thank Jeanie Thornblom, formerly coordinator of Library and Media Services at New Mexico Military Institute; Wesley Rusnell, registrar and curator of the Roswell Museum and Art Center; Donald Gallup, curator, Collection of American Literature at the Beinecke Rare Book and Manuscript Library at Yale, and his assistant Lisa Browar; Dennis McGuire and Andrew Bronstein, Connecticut Public Television; Donald Gray and his colleagues at the University of Northern Iowa Library; Gloria Jaramillo at the University of New Mexico's Zimmerman Library; Mr. Michael Q. Hooks, associate archivist of the Southwest Collection, Texas Tech University; Wes Wilson, Southwest Librarian, El Paso Public Library; Herbert Cahoon, curator, Autograph Manuscripts, the Pierpont Morgan Library; Elvis E. Fleming, archivist, the Chaves County Historical Society; Joan Jurale and Elizabeth A. Swaim, Olin Library, Wesleyan University; John W. Paton, University Editor, Wesleyan University; Jack Swickard and Lynne Vans of the *Roswell Daily Record*; Richard Pipes and Frankie McCarty of the *Albuquerque Journal*; Bobby Wayne Clark and Tom Pilkington; Horgan's friends and associates: Vincent Price; Frank Capra; John O. Crosby; Hugh Meglone Milton II; Henriette Wyeth Hurd; Leon Edel; Senator Daniel P. Moynihan; the Reverend Theodore M. Hesburgh, C.S.C.; Kit Reed; the late C. P. Snow and Lon Tinkle; Lawrence Clark Powell; Tom Kritser; Karl Detzer; Dwight Hunter, Jr.; Dwight Starr; Margaret Duffield; Susan Wirth; Dorothy B. Hughes; Rogers Aston; Mrs. Charles Henderson; E. W. Bisett; Colonel George W. Weego; Mrs. Robert H. Pearson; Virginia Hervey McElhany; Donald Winston; Sue Saunders Graham; Lieutenant General James P. Riseley; P. H. Gratton; William S. Marshall; Constance Parry Knapp; Mrs. E. G. Cullum; Charlotte S. Murphy; Elyse Saunders Patterson; Mrs. John Walden Bassett; E. W. Mitchell; Clarence E. Hinkle; some of Paul Horgan's early students: Harold D. Dufek, Bill Daniels, and Hubert Guy; Horgan's close friends at the University of Iowa: Paul Engle and Baldwin and Georgia Maxwell; two New Mexican authors: T. M. Pearce and Fray Angelico Chavez; also Margaret L. Hartley and the *Southwest Review*; and colleagues at Northern Iowa who helped me gain needed time and travel funds: H. Ray Hoops, Margarette Eby, and Jan Robbins; graduate assistant Evelyn Richardson; and two fine typists Lois Pittman and Debra Pressley. Professor W. Turrentine Jackson and the National Endowment for the Humanities took me West at a crucial time. I especially want to thank Mike, Maureen, Jack, and Mary Oates—and my own parents; and I owe much to Paul Horgan for his ever-willing cooperation and assistance during a marathon interview, several phone conversations, and in many letters. Permission to quote from Horgan's works has been granted by Farrar, Straus and Giroux. The photograph of Paul Horgan is by William Van Saun. Finally, I want to thank Janet Quimby, Emily McKeigue, and Kenneth Eble for invaluable editorial advice.

Chronology

1903 Paul Horgan born in Buffalo, New York, 1 August. Full baptised and confirmed name: Paul George Vincent O'Shaughnessy Horgan.

1915 Moves to Albuquerque, New Mexico, for father's health (tuberculosis). Attends Albuquerque public schools.

1916 Meets Francis, Erna, and Harvey Fergusson.

1919 Cadet, New Mexico Military Institute, Roswell, New Mexico. Meets Peter Hurd as fellow cadet.

1921 Reporter, *Albuquerque Journal.* Father died; mother stricken with lethargic encephalitis.

1922 Returns to New Mexico Military Institute, first year junior college.

1923 Returns to Buffalo, New York. Enters Eastman School of Music, Rochester, New York.

1924 June, "Exotics," in *Poetry Magazine.*

1926 Librarian, New Mexico Military Institute. Secretary for Witter Bynner, Santa Fe (summer).

1929 December, first short story, "The Head of the House of Wattleman," *Yale Review.*

1931 *Men of Arms* (juvenile), first book.

1933 *The Fault of Angels*, wins Harper Prize Novel Contest.

1935 *No Quarter Given.*

1936 *Main Line West; The Return of the Weed; From the Royal City.*

1937 *A Lamp on the Plains; New Mexico's Own Chronicle.*

1938 *Far From Cibola.*

1939 *The Habit of Empire.*

1940 *Figures in a Landscape.*

1942 *The Common Heart; A Tree on the Plains; Death, Mr. President.* Captain United States Army, General Staff Corps.

1946 Leaves army as lieutenant colonel. Lectures in Writers Workshop, University of Iowa (spring semester).

1947 Assistant to president, NMMI. Receives Guggenheim Fellowship.

1952 *The Devil in the Desert; One Red Rose for Christmas.*

1954 *Great River; Humble Powers.*
1955 Pulitzer and Bancroft prizes awarded for *Great River; The Saintmaker's Christmas Eve.*
1956 *The Centuries of Santa Fe.*
1957 *Give Me Possession.* Meets Igor Stravinsky.
1958 Second Guggenheim Fellowship.
1959 *Rome Eternal.*
1960 Fellow, Center for Advanced Studies, Wesleyan University. *A Distant Trumpet.*
1961 *Citizen of New Salem.* Fellow, Center for Advanced Studies.
1962 Director, Wesleyan Center for Advanced Studies. *Mountain Standard Time.*
1963 *Conquistadors in North American History; Toby and the Nighttime* (juvenile).
1964 *Things as They Are*; movie adaptation of *A Distant Trumpet.*
1965 *Peter Hurd: A Portrait Sketch from Life; Songs After Lincoln.*
1966 *Memories of the Future.*
1967 Resigns, director, Wesleyan Center for Advanced Studies. Adjunct professor of English, Wesleyan University. *The Peach Stone.*
1968 *Everything to Live For.*
1969 Professor of English and Permanent Author in Residence, Wesleyan University.
1970 *The Heroic Triad; Maurice Baring Restored; Whitewater.* Horgan Library dedicated, NMMI, Roswell.
1972 *Encounters with Stravinsky.*
1973 *Approaches to Writing*
1975 *Lamy of Santa Fe.*
1976 Pulitzer Prize for *Lamy.* Notre Dame's Laetare Medal.
1977 *The Thin Mountain Air.*
1979 *Josiah Gregg and His Vision of the Early West.*
1980 *Henriette Wyeth; The Return of the Weed* reissued.
1982 *Mexico Bay.*

Chapter One

True Humanist

Paul Horgan is a true humanist. He reveres the spiritual, intellectual, and aesthetic capabilities of mankind. He accepts humanity as it is, with all its beauty and blemish, and he affirms it. Such an attitude is easily enough inferred from his writings, from hearing his voice in his narrators and characters. When one begins to consider the body of his work as fictionist, historian, biographer, essayist, poet, "composer," and "maker"; considers his life as writer, painter, amateur musician, Catholic, teacher, librarian, soldier, patron, and administrator of the arts—when one considers the relationships between his art and life, one is left with no better designation of attitude and accomplishment than that of humanist. In 1968 Horgan said in honor of Edmund Wilson, "The true humanist is always polymath—always versatile . . ."; and in this sense Horgan himself is a true humanist.[1] Moreover, Jacques Maritain's definitions of "true humanism" and "integral humanism" also apply to Horgan when one assumes that "humanism . . . essentially tends to render man more truly human and make his original greatness manifest by causing him to participate in all that can enrich him in nature and in history. . . ."[2]

In terms of Horgan's definition of a true humanist or of Maritain's, tracing his humanism through his life and work is rewarding. The list of his awards and honors almost matches the length of the "provisional bibliography" of his work compiled in 1973 by James Kraft.[3] At the time of this writing, both honors and writings have increased yearly by significant numbers. Horgan's early self and audience have changed with the times; and current issues of populism, elitism, and ethnicity surround not only his humanistic assumptions but his portrayals of Hispanics and Native Americans. Thus Horgan's career as an author has within it a certain degree of controversy.[4]

The concern here is with Horgan as American author—with his writings much more than his biography. But, part of the present study's intention is to relate his life to his work, his beliefs and values to his art. This is not to blindly commit new criticism's "biographical fallacy" which places the author's life center stage in all he writes. Nor is it to carelessly attribute motive or intention. Horgan is keenly adept at distancing himself, through an obvious coloring of intuition and imagination, through what he has called a portraitist's "protean persona," from his fiction.

Even so, seeing Horgan's life is greatly relevant to seeing his art. Susan Wirth, who has devoted considerable time to investigating Horgan's genealogy, observes, "many of his novels have a strong biographical lilt. Some situations are directly taken, . . . from a real life situation."[5] This is no great revelation in that authors draw on their experience.

Nevertheless, understanding certain aspects of his biography highlights the importance of biography as genre and the general biographical dimension in all of his writings. Although the point is not argued exclusively, a thesis of the present appraisal is that Horgan's humanism is recognizable in broad biographical ways in his work. Such a perspective on his writings, amid all their variety of form and type and mode, admittedly stretches the boundaries of biography. Such a reading of Horgan looks at the author's biography, his life and times, his attitude of affirmation, in relation to the biographies he presents—biographies of both people and place. This is only one way to read him and perhaps it is simultaneously commonplace and daring. Assuredly, any mode or genre can be defined so broadly that meaning and significance are lost. But insofar as style is the man, then maybe literature and history are biography—or so Horgan tempts us to believe in his illuminations of lives and landscapes, of humanity and its heroes and heroines "of occasions."

Often regarded as a regionalist, an author of the American Southwest, Horgan is actually more transcontinental than local. The East and the West both play a large part in the transcontinental cycle of his career and in his books. The Mid-Atlantic states are as much a part of Horgan as is the Southwest. In this sense, he is a Yankee plainsman and projects this image into his writing. Although he spent many of his formative years in the West, it was in the East that he was born and the East to which he returned in his maturity, settling finally in New England. This transcontinental perspective common to Horgan penetrates what he writes. The East/West and West/East confrontation is in itself a central subject for him.

If writers have early, middle, and late phases, Horgan's may be designated East-West-East. His writing also falls neatly into a pre–

World War II and a post–World War II scheme—two careers. In the decade between his first published book in 1931 and his entering the Army in 1942, he wrote a dozen books and numerous short stories, reviews, and miscellaneous pieces—enough to say that the war halted his career as a writer for four years. The second phase of Horgan's career did not begin until the publication of *Great River* in 1954—making a twelve-year gap between published books. Blessed with a long life and much to write about, Horgan's career continued into later phases past other wars. But his life and career are too varied and complex to reduce to early and late, novelist or historian. A more comprehensive way of schematizing his life and career is by means of where he lived and what those regions meant to him. His "autobiographical" writings—aside from his novels—are found primarily in four works: *Peter Hurd: A Portrait Sketch From Life* (1965); *Encounters With Stravinsky* (1972); *Approaches To Writing* (1973); and *Henriette Wyeth* (1980).[6] "On Becoming an Artist," might be a subtitle to all of these writings.

East

Born on 1 August 1903 in Buffalo, New York, Paul George Vincent O'Shaughnessy Horgan spent the first years of his childhood in Buffalo until, at the age of twelve, he emigrated West, becoming, as Horgan says, a Westerner by "biographical accident."[7] The son of a close-knit Irish German family, Paul, his elder brother Edward (1901–) and his younger sister Rosemary (1906–49) had known enough of life in upper New York state to cherish its amenities before leaving for the more austere "frontier" of Albuquerque—then a small town in New Mexico which at the time of the Horgan family's move in 1915 was enjoying new statehood and an influx of tuberculosis and asthma patients looking for a new life. Edward Daniel Horgan (1871–1922), husband of Rose Marie Rohr Horgan (1873–1940), and father of the three Horgan children was such a patient. It was a move of mixed happiness and sorrow—one that, transformed in memory and imagination, appears in Horgan's fiction. In his life "myth" the West is a place of health and of exile.

In his Buffalo childhood home and in primary school at the French-Catholic Nardin Academy, Horgan's education and interest began to take on humanistic contours. The city of Buffalo contributed to his early sensibilities too, through its theaters, libraries, museums, musicians, and actors, its "general texture of cultivated social forms."[8]

Horgan's father was born in Oswego, New York, the son of John D. Horgan and Anna O'Shaughnessy Horgan, and soon moved with his parents to Elmira, New York. After graduating from business school in Buffalo, he worked for the Erie Railroad first in the loading department and later as a station manager in Binghamton, New York. In 1902 Horgan's father moved back to Buffalo and the employment of the Germania Life Insurance Company, and then, in 1905, in affiliation with Matthias Rohr (1840–1920), Paul Horgan's maternal grandfather, became vice-president and treasurer of the Volksfreund Printing Company. He was active in nearly a dozen civic and professional clubs in Buffalo and in that city "held a very good position and was well respected by everybody."[9] According to Horgan, by the time his father moved to New Mexico for his tuberculosis in 1915, he had made and saved enough money to more than partially provide for his wife after his death (H–1). This kind of prominence, which Edward Daniel Horgan, Sr., enjoyed and the tragedy of his death at the age of fifty-one, is reflected indirectly in the fictional characterizations of Richard's father, "Dan" throughout Horgan's "Richard trilogy"—with the travail of the New York to New Mexico move providing a real-life basis for the fictions of *The Thin Mountain Air* (1977).

Matthias Rohr also left a deep impression on Horgan. Born in the village of Zemmer in Rhenish Prussia he arrived in America in 1868, rapidly establishing himself as a journalist, poet, and businessman. Managing editor of the *Daily Volksfreund*, fluent in German, French, and English, devout in the Catholic faith, and well-known among the citizenry of Buffalo, Rohr wrote poems strong in pride for his German heritage. Matthias and Sophia Richert Rohr had eleven children, the third being Rose Marie, Paul Horgan's mother. The tenth was Paul Gonzaga Rohr (1885–1945), an uncle with a rather tragic life on whom Uncle Fritz seems modeled in the "Far Kingdoms" chapter of *Things as They Are* (1964), the first of the "Richard trilogy"—and the uncle after whom Paul Horgan might presumably have been named. Matthias Rohr seems to figure as Grosspa in the "Black Snowflakes" chapter of that novel.

The fourth child of Matthias and Sophia, Leo Maria Rohr (1875–97), drowned in the Flat Head Rapids of the Severn River in Canada and his body was never recovered. Similar drownings and near-drownings recur often enough in Horgan's writings to see the drowning of his uncle as a possible catalyst for such fictive imaginings. Of the other Rohr children who seem recognizable in the background of Horgan's fictions, mention should be made of Lucy, Clara, and Wilhelmina (Puss) who became nuns in the Franciscan order of the Sisters of Charity. *One Red Rose* (1951) comes to mind in this context in its story about the strong blood and spiritual bond between two nuns, Sister St. Anne and Mother Seraphim, who are also siblings. That story is dedicated to Marie Louise Rohr (1892–1977) who in her late years wrote many as yet unpublished words in reminiscence of her "esteemed nephew," Paul Horgan, and the Rohr-Horgan family.[10]

Under the tutelage of his grandfather, his German nurse, and his teachers at Miss Nardin's Academy, Horgan became a star pupil of German, one time winning a prize for sustaining conversation in German longer than his classmates (H–2). Family interest in music and art was keen: "Both sides of my family . . . had produced versatile and active amateurs in making music, painting water colors, reciting great poetry, taking delight in marvels of artistic performance" (*ES*, 4–5). Horgan studied the violin for a time, progressing far enough in those young days to play simplified portions of the Tschaikovsky concerto. Marie Rohr's memoirs are filled with instances of Horgan's parents' duets sung to piano accompaniment, of the masterful mimicry that his uncle Paul was capable of, as was the young Horgan who, it was soon discovered, could sing and, by the time he was seventeen, had a fine baritone voice. Small but elaborate family theatricals were the order of the day. Horgan recalls that he was writing and acting at an early age: "I was probably a pygmy writer in the nursery, beginning at let's say five or six. I remember a famous drama called 'The Innocent Fool.' . . . I would give it as a puppet show . . . , on a little tiny stage."[11]

If Buffalo left its imprint on Horgan's childhood, Rochester left its mark on his young adulthood. In 1923, two years after his father's death in New Mexico, Horgan moved back to New York and enrolled at the Eastman School of Music as a voice student. At Eastman he was a special student in voice and designed scenery for the opera department. In his second year at Rochester Horgan was appointed production assistant to Rouben Mamoulian who was director of the Eastman School of Dance and Dramatic Action. During that time Horgan sang and acted in several productions of the Eastman Theater. Horgan says, "My work under Mamoulian and my friendship with him was one of the most valuable and enlightening and inspiriting experiences of my life."[12] Exhausted from working twelve hours a day, Horgan left Rochester in 1926 to become librarian at the New Mexico Military Institute in Roswell where he had been a cadet—and to write daily, since he insisted on that provision before taking the job. James Kraft says about Horgan's Rochester years: "The experience was important, more in what he negated than what he affirmed."[13]

Horgan published his first poems while at Rochester and some of what he learned during those years showed up in extravagant productions at NMMI, in his folk-opera, *A Tree on the Plains* (1942), in *Death, Mr. President* (1942), and in the techniques involved in his writings. His first published novel, *The Fault of Angels* (1933), his first published short story, "The Head of the House of Wattleman" (1929), many of his shorter sketches for the *New Yorker* and other periodicals during the 1930s, and his personal essay "How Dr. Faustus Came to Rochester" (1936), all deal with his Rochester years. Much in Horgan's second published novel, *No Quarter Given* (1935), also builds on these experiences and in more subtle ways so do his other novels—whenever he calls upon his talents to "stage a scene."

Always drawn to writing poetry and short stories, his next destined influence was to be West—in a town known as "The Pride of the Pecos," a town he had known already and wanted to leave for the opportunities of the wider world. There, in Roswell, he would have to teach himself another craft for he knew nothing about being a librarian. But ever the autodidact, he was up to it. Like his father before him he headed West for health and a new start in different surroundings.

Vision on the shores of Lake Erie was not the vision of the prairies, mesas, mountains, and sky surrounding the Rio Grande and Pecos river valleys. Horgan taught himself in such a landscape to be an author with a double and somehow stronger perspective of a Yankee plainsman. In addition to the heroes and heroines represented by his family and by the musicans and actors at Eastman, he would reconcile Toscanini and Beethoven with Josiah Gregg and Jean Baptiste Lamy.

West

The West as it affected Horgan's life can be thought of as New Mexico, California, and Iowa. New Mexico was by far the greatest influence, its climate, landscape, and people—and three cities: Albuquerque, Roswell, and Santa Fe. A consideration of Horgan in these places tells much about his life and work, especially during the four decades between 1915 and 1960.

When the Horgan family moved to Albuquerque in 1915, it was not the metropolis it is at present. It was not Buffalo either. It was, however, a place in the sun, a high, dry altitude with "thin mountain air," a place to seek health for pulmonary patients like Horgan's father. Bounded on the east by the Sandia and Manzano mountains and on the west by extinct volcanoes, with the Rio Grande coursing through a wide trough of cottonwoods between the mountains and the volcanoes, and populated by three distinctive cultures of Hispanics, Anglo-Americans, and Native Americans, Albuquerque was an enchanting new world. In the biography of Albuquerque Horgan's own biography was mixed and in its lives and landscapes were the impressions which combined with other New Mexican towns to emerge in nearly forty books, countless stories, and numerous articles about the West.

Horgan speaks in terms of culture shock and gradual acceptance when he recalls his arrival in Albuquerque: "Moving to Albuquerque . . . I felt alien there until the magic of the country overcame me, and that took a year or two" (H–1). As Horgan told one Albuquerque interviewer, the city of his boyhood ended at the water reservoir on the campus of the University of New Mexico,[14] but his imagination soared much beyond.

Almost as important as the Rio Grande and the scale and grandeur of the country in Horgan's growing acceptance of Albuquerque was his friendship with the H. B. Fergusson family. The Fergussons proved that there were humanistic values and civilization like the Horgans had known in Buffalo to be found among the sandstorms, mesas, and arroyos of Albuquerque. Such an oasis of Anglo-American civilization in the "primitive" Southwest appears in various settings and characters throughout Horgan's writings. He says this about the influence of the Fergussons: "The whole Fergusson family were to me a great resource, endless refreshment and enrichment in life—all so adult, all so warm and charming, civilized, deeply, deeply civilized" (H–1).

Francis Fergusson, the youngest brother, was Horgan's contemporary. With Francis he explored the town and the river, especially that part of the river near the great house, a so-called "castle," built by Francis's grandfather, Franz Huning, one of the early founders of immigrant Albuquerque. Horgan's short story "A Castle in New Spain" (1940) and the character of Anton Zahm seem based on

Huning Castle and Franz Huning. Much of the locale of *The Common Heart* (1942) also takes place around the Huning Highlands, Albuquerque's first subdivision associated with newcomers from the East who bypassed indigenous architecture.[15]

In the early 1930s Horgan reviewed Harvey Fergusson's *Rio Grande* and Erna Fergusson's *Dancing Gods* and *Fiesta in Mexico* for the *Yale Review.* And in 1973 Horgan wrote an introduction to a reissue of Erna's *New Mexico.* That essay is a reminiscence of Horgan's friendship with Erna and a tribute to her. Here again civility in Albuquerque is equated with the Fergussons: "of all those [households] I knew in Albuquerque I felt most directly in touch with the graces of civilized life and the possibility of growth in those directions of the arts and ideas to which I was then aspiring as an adolescent."[16] Statements like this suggest that Erna Fergusson or her counterpart in Roswell, Mrs. Barry Duffield, turned up as fictionalized heroines. Southwestern author T. M. Pearce says, "[Horgan] was very close to Erna Fergusson. He loved Erna. I feel sure she's Victoria Cochran in *Whitewater.*"[17]

Besides the Fergussons, another important Albuquerque influence on Horgan was Clinton P. Anderson. In 1921–22 Anderson was city editor of the *Albuquerque Journal* (later Anderson was a New Mexico senator). It was the year of Horgan's father's death and the beginning of his mother's struggle with lethargic encephalitis. In the fall of 1921 he left NMMI where he was attending school, returned to Albuquerque, and found a job as a junior reporter under Anderson.

Due to his own bravado, and the good-humored free rein allowed by Anderson, Horgan learned the ins and outs of Albuquerque and of the small-town newspaper business. In addition to general office work and reporting, he was music, art, literary and dramatic critic, book reviewer, and follower of events in high society and city hall (H–2).

Reading Horgan's *Journal* pieces today it is easy to see why they got him into trouble. He was a precocious young journalist and only such a talented, literate teenager could be forgiven his daring and affectation. His most notorious piece bears the heading, "Last Flurry of June Brides Make Exit in Heat," which he wrote for the Sunday Social Section. He spends three-hundred words talking about vacations and hot weather diversions, alternating casual and formal levels of diction—intending to parody the very column he has been assigned to write as well as the society column of the rival evening *Tribune.*

A few sentences reveal why some readers angrily called the paper and the publisher threatened to fire him: "Some very stunning bathing frocks have been exhibited and the most popular . . . under certain safe conditions seems to be flesh."[18]

Horgan's experiences as a youth in Albuquerque fused the humanistic refinements of friendships with the Fergussons and Anderson and the local concerns written about in the *Journal* with the cultures of Native Americans and Hispanics. In his various "autobiographical" writings and interviews, snippets of other influential happenings are found, events that later entered into his writing because they were part of his biography. Coloring it all was the individual and family suffering of watching a father die and a mother grow ill and realizing that the future remained, in anticipation and memory.

Critic and editor, Kyle Crichton, once said, "At the age of seventeen Mr. Horgan was the damnedest young man the Southwest had ever seen."[19] Roswell and NMMI contributed to the formation of Horgan's extraordinary versatility and talent at that young age. Much honored today in Roswell, Horgan spent his sophomore and junior high school years as a cadet at NMMI (1919–21), and one year (1922–23) in which he was allowed to combine his senior year in high school with the first year of junior college. In 1926 he returned to Roswell from Rochester, assumed his duties as librarian, and remained in that capacity until 1942 at which time he entered the Army. Following World War II and a semester teaching in Iowa City, Horgan moved back to Roswell in 1947 and resided there until his affiliation with Wesleyan University began in 1960.

Horgan, like Roswell, is regarded as the "pride" of the Pecos. In 1970 NMMI named its library after him. The Roswell Museum and Art Center established "The Horgan Gallery" in honor of his hard work on the museum's board of directors. It was in Roswell and in association with NMMI that he decided to become a writer, choosing between his talents as singer, painter, and actor. Not only did Horgan organize and build the NMMI library during his sixteen years as librarian, he also published his first dozen books which established him as one of the leaders of what is called the "Southwestern renaissance."

A military school seems an unlikely place for Horgan to pursue his nascent artistic and humanistic interests. His accounts of his cadet years at NMMI are tinged with slight disdain for some of the assumptions of military training, and a sense of surprise as to how he was "rescued" from a merciless Spartan life. He dramatizes some of the failings of such a school—seemingly patterned on NMMI—in *A Lamp on the Plains* (1937). But he also had fond feelings for the military and NMMI as seen in the lyrics he wrote to the school song, "The Old Post":

> We will remember Kaydets marching,
> We will remember Kaydets playing
> And bugles in the sunrise,
> All of our life
> Beneath blue skies. . . .[20]

Horgan continued to build upon the glories connoted in the image of "bugles in the sunrise" in a promotional account of the Institute done in 1932 for *New Mexico*, the state's recreational and highway magazine. In that article his thesis rang out loud and clear: "Let it be stated and set aside, . . . that New Mexico Military Institute stands first among the nation's schools of its class."[21]

He was not a cadet at this time. He was a faculty member, one of the class of 1924, and loyally sincere. The positive aspects (though not without satire) of the "color of life" at such a school as NMMI are present again in Horgan's later novel about Annapolis, *Memories of the Future* (1966), and in other writings about "men of arms," including his military Western, *A Distant Trumpet* (1960). Although a piece like "Bugles" is useful for insight into a period of Horgan's life, the great "popularity"[22] which Horgan said it enjoyed was probably most useful in recruiting cadets. Certainly Horgan's own cadet accomplishments are exemplary. He received a new cadet scholarship, was one of the top students of his class each year, was managing editor of the school magazine, the *Maverick*, drew sketches for the yearbook, the *Bronco*, was in charge of the color guard, and advanced in grade to first lieutenant. He played the part of General Fuller in the drama "The Guilty Parties" in 1922 and prepared and arranged settings for "The Whirlpool."[23]

The most important friendship and influence at NMMI was the one which began in 1919 between first-year cadet Horgan and second-year cadet Peter Hurd—two artistic humanists, aged fifteen: "We knew each other from the very first as fellow artists . . ." (*PH*, 15). At NMMI Horgan shared the secret of Hurd's homemade still; they collaborated on two serial novels entitled "The Silver Lamp" and "Gold";

and they shared Sunday lunches and Monday afternoon teas at the Hurd family home in Roswell (*PH*, 13–21). Hurd later did the illustrations for two of Horgan's books: lithographs for *The Return of the Weed* (1936) and wash drawings for *The Habit of Empire* (1938). Hurd also did the jackets of *Main Line West* (1936) and *The Common Heart* (1942). About Hurd's illustrations for *Weed* and *Empire* Horgan says, "I always felt that my text could just as well be considered as extensions of his vision as the other way round" (*PH*, 42). Horgan's friendship with Hurd meant much to both men. Like the Fergussons and C. P. Anderson in Albuquerque, the Horgan-Hurd Roswell connection nourished Horgan's humanism and humanity.

When Horgan returned to NMMI in 1926, after his three years in Rochester, it was as librarian. And for the next sixteen years, until 1942 when he joined the war effort first in the Information and Education Division and later in the Army's General Staff Corps, his objective was twofold: to develop the best library possible and to begin his career as a man of letters. The condition of his job as librarian was that he have mornings free to write. He wrote five novels before *Angels* (1933) was published and after winning the Harper Prize novel contest with that book he continued to publish regularly. Success as an author complemented his success as a librarian.

When he became librarian the books were arranged according to the color of binding and the holdings were numbered at 2,000 volumes. When he resigned as librarian in 1942 the library boasted 20,000 volumes, and at the time of the dedication of the Horgan Library, the holdings were at 52,000 volumes. The bronze sign outside the library identifies Horgan as musician, painter, novelist, dramatist, poet, biographer, historian, educator. Horgan's remarks, read by his brother in his absence, illustrate the role the library had in allowing him such varied humanistic pursuits: "The library was my early gateway to whatever education I can claim outside my brief classroom career, and I hope it will always be the medium of enlarged horizons for those who will come after us."[24]

Horgan says something of the same thing in *A Lamp on the Plains* (1937), about Roswell, NMMI, and libraries regardless of size. Two autobiographical essays which elaborate on Horgan's work as a librarian and his notions of librarian as humanist are *One of the Quietest Things* (1960) and "An Amateur Librarian" (1976).[25] For Horgan, the importance of a librarian and the use of a library go much beyond card catalog and alphabet. The values implicit are rather, "a consuming love for the faculty of man's mind, and an abiding respect for the reach of anyone toward any manifestation of it" (*OQ*, 9). The true librarian is a humanist.

One place where Horgan's librarianship and authorship converge is in a periodical he began called simply *The Library*. From 15 November 1926 until 15 May 1927 he edited and printed this "newsletter." *The Library* was one of many devices he used to stimulate an interest among the cadets in using the library. Aside from its contents, *The Library* reveals in its design his artist's eye, his pleasure in such things as typography, and his overall tastefulness. Horgan wrote close to thirty reviews, translations, and poems in his magazine—under his own name and initials and under his then sometime pen name of Vincent O'Shaughnessy. It was a period of much interest in poetry on his part, and the time of his poetic pamphlets, "Vilanelle of Evening" (a 1926 Christmas message of 200 copies), and "Lamb of God," (a poem in six stanzas, printed privately in a run of sixty copies in March 1927 and dedicated to Witter Bynner). Horgan was introduced to Witter Bynner by Erna Fergusson in 1926 and worked for him as secretary for a summer. *The Library* reflects this friendship.

The first issue features two poems by Bynner and in the following spring (15 May 1927), Bynner's "At Acoma" is featured. The first issue also serves, in a sense, to report on Horgan's summer working for Bynner—a summer which seems to have further initiated Horgan into the larger writer's world of Santa Fe. One notice reads: "During the past summer, the following writers were among those who visited the old city, some to work, some to play: Willa Cather, Edgar Lee Masters, Floyd Dell, Alfred Kreymborg and Paul Rosenfeld."[26]

In addition to reorganizing and strengthening the library's holdings through such ventures as his monthly magazine, Horgan's other duties at NMMI included coaching the tennis team, advising student publications, teaching, and designing elaborate sets for the graduation balls. As tennis coach he always challenged and usually beat his best player to illustrate that those who coach should also do. His 1935–36 team was the best in the school's history, winning the New Mexico Conference Championship.[27] One of Horgan's players recalls about his coach: "Aside from the expected mechanics of such an association, . . . he was inspirational; he was . . . a guiding light to young men who abruptly found themselves bound by rather severe restrictions of a military school."[28] Numerous other students testify in much the same terms to the inspirational effect Horgan had on their lives. As an example of how Horgan's humanist values carried beyond the classroom, in 1936–37 he founded the Beethoven Society where every weekend members would listen to recorded concerts in his quarters.[29] Horgan's efforts as consulting editor of *The Maverick* are everywhere seen in the Christmas 1930 issue, notably in the poem "Why and Wherefore of Billy the Kid."[30]

Extending his humanist interests to the community, Horgan did much in support of the Roswell Museum and Art Center. The Museum began in 1937 as a result of the combined efforts of the city of Roswell, the Chaves County Historical Society, and the Roswell Friends of Art. Horgan is credited with establishing the Southwestern Collection at the time of reorganization in 1949 when he became the first president of its board of trustees.[31] The Museum's Peter Hurd and Witter Bynner collections indirectly reflect Horgan's guidance of acquisitions. The letter of appreciation by the board of trustees to Horgan on his resignation in the spring of 1955 says in part that he helped create "a living museum which brings to our community aspects . . . of our local history and culture together with art treasures of our inherited world culture."[32]

In Horgan's mind the function of a museum is not unlike that of a library; they are extensions of our humanity, our civilization: "The supreme act of self-respect in any society is to know its own origins, gather all possible evidence for these, and share them with an interested public in a form as appropriate and beautiful as possible."[33]

In Roswell Horgan became part of a special literary regionalism. Journalist Lon Tinkle attributed much of the flowering of Southwestern writing in the 1930s and 1940s to the *Southwest Review*. Until World War II it was a major channel for the writings of J. Frank Dobie, John H. McGinnis, Paul Horgan, and others.[34] In Tinkle's account it was not so much a rebirth of Western writing but a birth: "Without friendships like Dobie's with McGinnis, the *naissance* might never have taken place. An artist needs some kindred spirits, and some precedents as well."[35] Horgan contributed five pieces to the *Southwest Review* in 1933, 1941, 1943, 1954, and 1955—all significant in whatever awakening there was and especially important to Horgan's own developing body of work. His 1933 essay, "About the Southwest: A Panorama of Nueva Granada," is the most important because from it grew a broader "panorama" of other works.[36] Lawrence Clark Powell does not speak in terms of a renaissance so much as he does of a "great constellation" of Southwestern writers and artists and calls Horgan the dean of Southwestern writers.[37]

Horgan acknowledges that there was a Southwestern renaissance and credits the *Southwest Review* with part of it. He tells about his meeting McGinnis in the fondest of terms because McGinnis thought enough of *Angels* and its success to drive from Dallas to Roswell to congratulate him (*AW*, 225–27). Horgan believes that Santa Fe had perhaps more to do with such a renaissance than anything, in that painters and writers began to descend on that town in the early 1920s. As for his own role in such a movement, he says, "If I'm a part of the Southwestern renaissance it's just because of the time. It wasn't because of any association or influence either way" (H–1).

Choosing not to be regarded as a regionalist writer, Horgan says, "I'm not like any other Southwestern writer I know" (H–1), and says that his Roswell residence—early and middle phases—was a lucky one because of the independence it allowed him: "I was able to search for my own way, alone, however deviously" (*AW*, 220). The art colonies of Taos and Santa Fe were at first accepted uncritically by him. In his earliest years in New Mexico they particularly had their value for they enabled a youthful artist "to breathe a climate and absorb justification for his own socially unorthodox values" (*AW*, 221). But settled as a writer in Roswell from 1926 until 1942, and again from 1947 until 1962, some of the northern colonists in Taos and Santa Fe came to seem "somewhat grotesque, self-advertising, and responsive to opportunities for envy and competition" (*AW*, 221). All in all, Horgan much preferred Santa Fe to Taos. Some of this sentiment turns up in "So Little Freedom" (1942) where Horgan sympathetically portrays D. H. Lawrence and satirizes Mabel Dodge Luhan in the guise of the boring Mrs. Gerald Boree.

In addition to Albuquerque and Roswell, Santa Fe is an important New Mexico place in Horgan's life and writing. Horgan never lived in Santa Fe permanently although he stayed there temporarily at various times into the early 1960s. A glance at a few of the titles of Horgan's books show the fascination Santa Fe holds for him: *From the Royal City* (1936), *Centuries of Santa Fe* (1956), and *Lamy of Santa Fe* (1975). Horgan first visited Santa Fe as a boy; saw Cather, and met Bynner and other friends there; helped to get the Santa Fe Opera underway; "enountered" Stravinsky—in short, found a great sense of "civilization" there.

Witter Bynner (1881–1968) was a central literary personage in Santa Fe during the 1920s and until his death. According to Santa Fe author, Dorothy B. Hughes, Bynner was a popular host: "It was at his museum-piece house that one met all the writers and artists and VIPs who visited Santa Fe."[38] Horgan's notice in *The Library* lists many of these. Among the local artists and writers who were part of Bynner's inner circle were Haniel Long, Lynn Riggs, Frank Applegate, Willard Nash, Andrew Dasburg, Randall Davey, Alice Corbin, and occasionally Mabel Dodge Luhan.

Oliver La Farge's *Santa Fe: The Autobiography of a Southwestern Town*, for which Horgan wrote the foreword, records some of the feeling of the Santa Fe of that period. Bynner is indexed many times, indicating that the local newspaper, the *New Mexican*, often reported his role in making the town a kind of humanistic crossroads in a then very remote region. As Horgan describes it, "Santa Fe is a city of junctions and arrivals—many cultures and historical traditions meet there."[39]

In addition to the books Horgan wrote as part of the Southwestern Renaissance between his return to Roswell in 1926 and his entering the Army in 1942 (including seven novels, three volumes of short stories, a small "biography" of soldiers, and a history text), he published twenty or so stories and essays in at least a dozen magazines; poetry in *Poetry* magazine; long critical and biographical pieces on Josiah Gregg, Witter Bynner, and George Washington; a play and a folk opera; and he wrote for many smaller regional publications, including *Laughing Horse: A Magazine of the Southwest*, published in Taos and edited by Willard Johnson; the *New Mexico Quarterly*, edited by T. M. Pearce; and the *New Mexico Sentinel*, published in Santa Fe by Cyrus McCormick, with a "New Mexico Writers" page edited by Haniel Long—with Horgan, Bynner, and Erna Fergusson as associates. Moreover, Horgan appeared in Southwestern anthologies edited by Alice Corbin, T. M. Pearce, Telfair Hendon, B. A. Botkin, and others. Beyond the renaissance of Southwestern writing before World War II, Horgan continued well into the second half of the century not just as a New Mexico author but as a significant contributor to the development of American literature.

The West and New Mexico remain Horgan's greatest biographical and artistic stimulus during his early, middle, and late phases. The West has always stayed with him and even though he resides in Connecticut he returns yearly to New Mexico—to visit the Hurds in San Patricio and Roswell friends like Mr. and Mrs. Robert O. Anderson; for the Santa Fe Opera; and for the inspiration provided by the spirit of place, by geography and the interaction of Native American, Hispanic, and Anglo cultures. The fact that his recent novel, *The Thin Mountain Air* (1977), has New Mexico as its primary setting, is indicative of the West's lingering influence on Horgan.

California and Iowa play a lesser role in the Western phases of Horgan's life and work than the New Mexico cities of Albuquerque, Roswell, and Santa Fe. But they are worth mentioning because they were temporary residences and provide settings for his writings.

Although Horgan visited California many times, he never stayed longer than nine or ten months at one time. And this was when he was in the Army working on a film under Frank Capra, who remained a close friend after the war. Horgan does not claim to have much more than a visitor's awareness of California (H–3); but the impressions he had there were strong ones and he used them in *Give Me Possession* (1957) and *Memories of the Future* (1966). Several of Horgan's short stories like "National Honeymoon" (1950) also build on California impressions and settings.

When Horgan left the Army in January 1946 he went to Iowa City and taught in the Graduate School of Letters at the University of Iowa. Paul Engle says, "He was such a good teacher as well as writer, I invited him to teach on the Writers Workshop staff when I became Director; he had an office up in a tower of the . . . 'Old Armory' building . . . where he wrote."[40] Horgan was hired to teach as a visiting lecturer during the second semester.[41] Among the twenty-nine students with whom Horgan worked in course 108 was Flannery O'Connor. O'Connor recounts: "At Iowa, I was only a student and Horgan never even knew I was in the room, I am sure—though once he noted forty things wrong with a story of mine and I thought him a fine teacher."[42] In Horgan's memory, "The one student I had who later made an important name was Flannery O'Connor; but I hasten to add I don't think I taught her much. She was already an artist—really an enigma, and a painfully shy person" (H–1). A small part of *A Distant Trumpet* (1960) is traceable to Horgan's semester in Iowa City. He also worked on *Memories of the Future* (1966), bridging the artistically vacant war years with the new impetus his writing would take with the major project he ached to begin, a history of the Rio Grande.

East

A somewhat idyllic prewar place in the East for Horgan, a place that is the basis for the settings of *Everything to Live For* (1968) and the story "The Burden of Summer" (1932), among others, is Chadds Ford, Pennsylvania, the home of painter N. C. Wyeth and his family. After Peter Hurd married Henriette Wyeth, N. C. Wyeth's daughter, Horgan visited them at Chadds Ford several times. The entire Brandywine Valley and all of the Wyeths had a lasting effect on Horgan. The elder Wyeth, as a teacher of his children and Peter Hurd, also devoted some time to criticizing and encouraging Horgan in his early writing (*ES*, 62). N. C. Wyeth, Henriette Wyeth, Andrew Wyeth, and Peter Hurd are all subjects of biographical appreciations by Horgan.

Horgan's war years were spent at the Pentagon as chief of the Army Information Branch of the Information and Education Division. Of the many branches of the division, the Information Branch was the largest and most far-reaching. As "the biggest publisher in the world" for three and a half years Horgan thought the job to be a sympathetic one and felt lucky to be assigned to it. Today Horgan speaks with a sense of gratitude and liking about his military service—an attitude that carries over into his fiction, into the characterization of his numerous military heroes where duty, in many forms, becomes a supreme value.

Aside from the story, "Old Army," which was published in the *Saturday Evening Post* (February 1944), Horgan's other notable war publication is a booklet on venereal disease, *You Don't Think . . .* (1944), published by the Government Printing Office. Once the booklet was approved by the Surgeon General's office and went into print, it ran two or three million copies and, ironically, set the record for Horgan's most widely read work.

Horgan thinks of his years in Washington as "confining but useful," something "to which in all conviction I was able to give my entire energy" (*ES*, 72). His prescription for an officer on his Pentagon staff reads like this: "Imagination, toughness, energy, wit (which is of the mind) and humor (of the gut), absolute dedication to the job of the war, and a sense of privilege in fighting for it."[43] He tried to follow that prescription himself, leaving the Army as a lieutenant colonel, and awarded the Legion of Merit. Even in war time he maintained his humanist ideals.

Horgan's main residence in the East, the one that completed his East-West-East life pattern, is Connecticut and Wesleyan University. Here his early Mid-Atlantic phase of Buffalo, Rochester, and Chadds Ford resolved into New England and a general Eastern seaboard ambiance. He says, "The pattern of my life seems to be complete in my coming back to the East, without at all losing the Southwest. I still have to be there frequently. Aesthetically I love it. But this kind of life [at Wesleyan] is very satisfying" (H–1).

He first went to Wesleyan for an honorary doctorate in 1956 at the invitation of President Victor L. Butterfield, a man who proved a persuasive influence. Horgan returned again in 1960 as one of the first Fellows at Wesleyan's new Center for Advanced Studies and spent another semester there in 1961. In 1962 he was asked to become its director, a position which, like his other administrative posts at NMMI and the Pentagon, he took on with total dedication. Although he feared to leave New Mexico, it was a prestigious career opportunity not to be denied. In 1965 he was named Hoyt Fellow, Saybrook College, at Yale. Then, following his resignation from the directorship of the Center in 1967, he became adjunct, then professor of English—and in 1971 he was given emeritus rank and named Permanent Author in Residence.

Horgan's teaching at Wesleyan was limited to a small number of students, working in depth with literature, history, and writing. Some of the courses he taught include a course in Southwestern history based on *Great River*; a seminar with tutorials in creative writing; and a course in writing biography.[44] Describing his life at Wesleyan in retirement as Author in Residence he says, "My life here consists of working in this room [library-study] . . . , and seeing students when I can, when they can see me—a very limited social life here with faculty friends; a kind of environment which is so different from New Mexico. . . . I would say that the amenities are more generally common in this area."[45]

Horgan never married and now approaching eighty and in good health, except for arthritis and a pesky skin condition due to so many years in the New Mexico sun, he lives a quiet life on the Wesleyan campus in a picturesque converted carriage house with a library of some 10,000 books—most of them copiously annoted by his pencil. On the walls are paintings by Peter Hurd, the Wyeths, and Horgan himself. He makes frequent trips with Wesleyan friends and others to museums and concerts in New York City and elsewhere. His green

Chevrolet Caprice convertible (one of the last "classic" ones made) shows the well-maintained use of a veteran traveler, deserving of the tastefully monogrammed doors. Between 1960 when he first became a Wesleyan Fellow, and continuing into 1983, he has published, on the average, a book a year.

As director of the Center for Advanced Studies, Horgan lived and administered a humanist's ideal. The Center existed from its founding in 1959 until 1969 when it was superseded by the Wesleyan Center for the Humanities. During those ten years the Center intended to combine the purposes of teaching students and adding to "the world's store of creative knowledge."[46] Each of the ten years found eight to sixteen gifted persons sharing in a series of Monday Night Papers the results of their work. Horgan developed friendships throughout these years with such Fellows as C. P. Snow, Ernst Bacon, Lewis Mumford, Edmund Wilson, Leon Edel, Daniel P. Moynihan, and many others. To them all Horgan said he owed "an enrichment in the faculties of affection and understanding, comradeship and spiritual ignition. . . ."[47]

Horgan's years at the Center may be viewed as a culmination of his best times in the intellectual, artistic, and humanist "centers" represented by the Fergussons and C. P. Anderson in Albuquerque; the Hurds in Roswell; the better moments of creativity and enlightenment at Roswell's military school and town museum and art center; the Santa Fe of Witter Bynner; the N. C. Wyeth family and home in Chadds Ford; even the movie making with Capra in Hollywood and the information writing at the Pentagon during World War II. As a true humanist Horgan revered humankind in the flesh and blood of friendship as well as in the ideal of the family of man. Across the country, East and West and East again, as both Yankee and plainsman, his interest seems always to have been in man's nature and in ways of enriching that nature—as a man and an artist.

Chapter Two

The Novels

Horgan's career as a novelist goes back fifty years to his first published Harper Prize novel, *The Fault of Angels*, in 1933. His career as a novelist continues into the last quarter of the century, to "postmodern" times, to the publication of his latest novel to date, *Mexico Bay* (1982), which makes him an interesting author to consider in light of the continuing "moral fiction" dialogue going on in American letters. If one sides with John Gardner and Gerald Graff on the issue, Horgan's resistance to fashionable movements for their own sake gains appreciation. Gardner argues that "art is essentially and primarily moral . . . art builds; it never stands pat; it destroys only evil. . . . This . . . is what true art is about—the preservation of the world of gods and men."[1] Graff defines postmodernism as "the movement within contemporary literature and criticism that calls into question the traditional claims of literature and art to truth and human value."[2] Clearly siding with the traditional realistic and moral claims of literature, Horgan's own views on morality and art are succinctly explained in his preface to *Humble Powers* (1954). To him an act of art and an act of piety are interconnected, both celebrating life: "there is no break in the circle when it encloses that motive which sees devotion in all acts that attempt to capture the likeness of life."[3]

Horgan's attempts to capture the likeness of life in art and in piety go much beyond the form of the novel and include shorter fiction, history, and biography—all written more or less simultaneously over the early, middle, and later phases of his career. Despite Pulitzer prizes for history-biography, it is as a novelist that Horgan is best known and as a novelist that probably he will make his most enduring mark as an artist. This is not to suggest that his novels exist in isolation from the rest of his writing. Quite the contrary—all of his writing in various genres is interrelated.

When considering Horgan the novelist it is easiest to follow his development from his beginnings before World War II, acknowledge the break in his career caused by the war, and then look at the novels he wrote after the war—realizing that his first major work after he resumed his postwar writing career was *Great River* (1954), his masterwork of historical biography. Before World War II Horgan wrote many works of shorter fiction which augmented his novels; after the war many of those stories were collected as the product of four decades of short stories in *The Peach Stone* (1967). Other shorter works of fiction including his well-known novellas *The Devil in the Desert* (1952) and *The Saintmaker's Christmas Eve* (1955) were at least in part the results of his research for *Great River.* But in all of Horgan's fiction one sees reflections of his nonfiction, echoes of his prewar works heard in what he wrote after the war.

It is too simple to say that Horgan's best novels were written before the war. Certainly the seven novels he published in the 1930s and early 1940s include some of his finest novels and evidence the finding of his voice, his *métiér.* These novels are *The Fault of Angels* (1933), *No Quarter Given* (1935), *Main Line West* (1936), *A Lamp on the Plains* (1937), *Far From Cibola* (1938), *The Habit of Empire* (1939), and *The Common Heart* (1942). Thematically and stylistically, *Angels* and *No Quarter*—his first two published novels—although different in tone, are companion novels and anticipate much of his other fiction, especially the postwar Richard trilogy. *Main Line West* and *A Lamp on the Plains* combine to follow two stages in the maturation of a single protagonist. *Cibola* and *The Common Heart,* in addition to anticipating *Whitewater* (1970), are masterpieces of form. In 1962, *Main Line West, Far From Cibola,* and *The Common Heart* were combined in a beautifully integrated trilogy, facilitated in part by Horgan's individual afterwords, entitled *Mountain Standard Time.* But even the lesser works of Horgan's beginnings as a novelist, such as *Empire,* may be linked together in a Peter Hurd-like prose mural of Anglo-American settlement along the rivers and on the plains of the great Southwest.

To be sure, Horgan's prewar novels stand on their own. However, in them too may be seen the basis for potential fully realized in his most successful and seasoned postwar novels: his classic military Western, *A Distant Trumpet* (1960); the Richard trilogy: *Things as They Are* (1964), *Everything to Live For* (1968), and *The Thin Mountain Air* (1977); his latest novel, *Mexico Bay* (1982); and his most lyrical novel, *Whitewater* (1970). The two novels exclusively about World War II, *Give Me Possession* (1957) and *Memories of the Future* (1966), are the least satisfying of his novels written after the war. *Mexico Bay*, less about wartime Washington, D.C., than the Texas gulf area, marks a culmination to and synthesis of his postwar novels.

Beginnings

Horgan's first two published novels, *The Fault of Angels* (1933) and *No Quarter Given* (1935), may be read as companion novels—one comic and set in the East; one tragic with an East/West tension. They may also be read as fictionalized biographies of Horgan and his experiences as a young man and artist in New York and New Mexico. Whether or not readers choose to draw parallels with Horgan's own biography, both of these novels, like the later Richard trilogy, are *Künstlerromans*, portraits of the artist as a young man. As such, their method of narration is biographical and autobiographical. His subsequent novels are incipient in the social satire and moral realism of these early novels.

Before he was a published novelist, Horgan wrote five novels which he tells about in *Approaches to Writing.* All of these early, never-published attempts at novels were satirical and he lists as some of his influences on his fourth try, "The Golden Rose" (the manuscript of which has survived and is at Yale), such authors as Carl Van Vechten, Max Beerbohm, and Ronald Firbank. Into the portrait of his heroine, Madame Maimonides, and her ambition for earning the papal award of a golden rose, was an attempt at satirical humor (*AW*, 214).[4] Underneath the frivolity, however, was a serious purpose. And this holds true for the other four early novels of his apprenticeship, none of them extant: "The Furtive Saint," "The Grey Swans," "Jupiter, A Novel," and "Death Insupportable" (*AW*, 192–219). Though each novel was rejected by publishers during the 1920s, Horgan nevertheless persevered.

Simultaneously with his flourish of interest in satire was an interest in the preoccupation of the 1920s and the 1930s with "realism." He describes that time of his apprenticeship as one "when a proletarian 'realism' was in energetic charge of intellectual life, probably given its chance by the miseries of the Great Depression" (*AW*, 218). Serious satire converged with the moral and ethical issues implicit in the depression years, and with Horgan's developing sense of place and region. Resisting any narrow definition of "realism," Horgan made accommodations of his own, reconciling his interests with those of the prevalent literary mood: "life at any level and in any circumstances is 'real' and 'realism' can justly encompass it" (*AW*, 218). Horgan's stance as satirist-realist was set in this 1920s apprenticeship and in his first two published novels he was hailed a success as a "beginning" novelist beyond his most hopeful expectations. His beginnings matured during the decade of the 1930s until the interruption of World War II.

The Fault of Angels. *Angels* (1933) is significant for many reasons, primarily because, as Horgan says, "It was the first of my full-length works to sound like myself" (*AW*, 223). It was a voice which had its nurturing in the musical world of Rochester; a voice which fused satire and comedy with the realism of one who had been a part of that scene, those lives: "It was a comedy—some said 'high comedy'—and its theme led to Russian tears and futility, but in its course the story brought the reader a feeling of reality, for it was compounded of elements all of which I myself had known well . . ." (*AW*, 223).

The announcement of the Harper Prize for 1933 reached Horgan on his thirtieth birthday. The prize carried an award of $2,000 outright and $5,000 minimum guarantee of royalties. Sinclair Lewis, one of the judges in the contest, said it was one of the first American novels which portrayed the arts in a provincial city. (Lewis's liking of *Angels* was probably boosted by the compliment paid to him in the novel as an author all Europeans "admired wildly," one who is imitated in a game called "short stories" and is easily recognized by Horgan's characters.)[5] Lewis's *Main Street* (1920) and *Babbitt* (1922) and their provincial cities had, somewhat similarly, anticipated *Angels.*

Reviewers echoed the favorable vote of Lewis. One reviewer stopped short of calling it a first-rate novel because of long-windedness but said Horgan "has exploited a fresh and bizarre vein of native American material."[6] Edward Cornelius said *Angels* made clear that "the material for social satire in America is superabundant."[7] Clifton Fadiman said Horgan's attempt in the novel was "To depict, in terms half ironic, half sentimental, the contours of the 'cultivated' society in a medium-sized American city. . . ."[8] Alfred Carter chose not to see the novel as satire, saying it was "rich in resources that save it from the general classification of 'satire,' although it is ironical in its treatment of American arts and their devotees."[9] Thirty years after the novel's publication, James M. Day believes that *Angels* is neither typical of Horgan's novels or expressive of "true humor"; though he does describe it as "a comedy of manners dealing with the efforts of the provincial town of Dorchester to establish local 'culture'."[10]

Whatever the degree of comedy and realism in *Angels*, it is related to Horgan's experiences at the Eastman School of Music. Many of the anecdotes surrounding the "legend" of the novel point to this, as does one of the central characters in the novel, John O'Shaughnessy. (O'Shaughnessy is both a family and a pen name for Horgan.) Readers in Rochester and at Eastman spotted O'Shaughnessy as a transparent persona for Horgan and saw themselves and familiar places. Horgan recounts that he was not "officially restored" to the favor of Rochester until almost forty years later in 1971 when the Friends of the Rochester Public Library gave him their annual literary award (*AW*, 229). If so inclined, through reading *Approaches* and *Encounters*, and "How Dr. Faustus Came to Rochester," one can match up the fictive and real personages. Probably it is advisable to regard the characters in *Angels* as composites of people he knew and of Horgan himself.

At the allusive center of the novel is Alexander Pope's satire, *The Dunciad.* Martin Price observes that the westward movement in *The Dunciad* "is the ironic counterpart of Aeneas' bearing the culture of alien Troy to Latium, to found a new empire which would culminate in the Augustan Age of Virgil."[11] Such a mission is the outline for much of the novel's tension as the heroine, Nina Arenkoff, ambitiously attempts to bring her humanism of the heart to what she sees as the materialistically motivated cultural enterprises of the wealthy patron and community patriarch of Dorchester, Henry Ganson. (Dorchester is Horgan's convention for Rochester and Buffalo.) Nina is described by her friend, Blanche Badger, in her attempts to convert Ganson to her values, as having what Pope called the "fault of angels": "Ambition first sprung from your bless'd abode; / The glorious fault of angels and of gods" (*FA*, 69).

Nina's ambitious assault on Ganson and Dorchester is the basis of the plot which revolves around Nina's arrival in Dorchester, her stay, and her departure for Paris. It is Nina's story, and John's. Nina's comings and goings, and the entrances and exits of other characters are staged in such a way as to make the novel seem like a theatrical production.

In the first chapters the reader awaits with suspense, as does John, the arrival of Madame Arenkoff, intuiting that she will control everyone's attention. Horgan achieves this through the awareness of John who will receive Nina into his experience, introduce her to Dorchester, fall in love with her, and suffer to see her leave, considering for a brief moment to go with her.

Nina's arrival is preceded by John's arrival as factotum for the production staff of the Ganson Theater and by the arrival of Nina's husband, Vladimir Arenkoff, who wins out as conductor of the orchestra over a man of more popular tastes, the American George Lane Doore. As John helps Val Arenkoff find an apartment and await Nina's arrival, much of the cast of the Ganson Theater parade by the reader: the philanthropic old bachelor, Henry Ganson; Cyril Derik, the English director of the theater; Hubert Regis, English guest conductor of the Dorchester Philharmonic Orchestra; George Doore, whose ousting by Arenkoff places him in a villainous role; and Nicolai Savinsky and Colya, two of John's musician friends; Lydia, a close friend of John's from Buffalo and the first harpist of the orchestra; Blanche Badger, friend and socialite; Julie Rale, head of the vocal department at the Ganson music school; Mrs. Leona Schrantz, the Arenkoffs' landlady; and Mrs. Kane, her rich sister. Dorchester in 1924, like Rochester of the same period, is on the threshold of a cultural renaissance thanks to Ganson's school of music, his theater, and now with Val's appointment, the provincial opera. The catalyst is Nina, just the kind of flamboyant personage who seeks to bring meaning in human terms to the issues which the city's artistic debut portends. Soon the spotlight of gossip, snobbery, and social intrigue is directed at her. Far from shy, she is ready to act and react.

Nina is very much an artist. She makes beautiful objects through sewing and embroidering. She is an actress and an impersonator, excelling at character sketches, costuming, and mimcry. She is a purveyor of her own cosmopolitan brand of humanism and European culture which is at odds with Dorchester's provincialism. Horgan's repeated means of humorously identifying her involve caricaturizing her strongly accented Russian dialect, and her constant weeping over the sadness of life which she feels in America as an exile. She explains her "tristesse" to Blanche Badger after seeing the vanity displayed by Mrs. Kane: "Is for world I cry. . . . Is such a sick world, wiz la Kane like everyone else. All of America is zis way; is fault of so much money and so much ambition" (*FA*, 68). Finding no spiritual meaning to the general society in Dorchester, Nina laments, "dreadful, all zose money," and the narrator elaborates on her feeling, "no soul, no art, not even any manners. Life was composed of these things in sad misproportion" (*FA*, 68). As she goes from party to party, and as her program of changing Ganson gains momentum, Nina's social artistry, her greatest art, is everywhere felt. Her humanistic and humanitarian values are expressed in action as well as in words. This is seen most prominently when Nina claims responsibility for the socially ostracized landlady, Mrs. Schrantz, when she is murdered by her thwarted lover, George Works. Nina claims the landlady's body and arranges her funeral when Mrs. Kane refuses to make known that she is Mrs. Schrantz's sister. And it is Nina who rescues Martin Bliss, the son of John's landlady, by falsely confessing to a theft of which Martin is accused. With John's help, Nina sees that Bliss regains his job. She also attempts to bring Doore back into the good graces of John and his friends.

Contrasting Nina's involvement with the likes of a promiscuous landlady, a wronged store clerk, and a scoundrel like Doore (Doore too, it is revealed, is one of Leona's lovers and a witness to her murder), Nina also affects the lives of more prestigious personages. The most eminent personage affected by Nina is Ganson for he is at the center of her arrival, stay, and departure. He is the one character who is most identified with Dorchester. What Nina naively does not expect is that Ganson will fall in love with her in only three months time. Comically, in her success is her failure, for she succeeds in doing much more by way of reviving Ganson's soul and spirit than she had intended. Her recounting to John of Ganson's avowal of love is one of the most successfully funny scenes in the novel and provides a final motive for her to leave Dorchester for Paris.

But it is John who is most affected by Nina in the close friendship which develops between them—filled with strategic kisses and tempting enticements. There is no jealousy of Nina evidenced in her husband, Val, and he remains in John's eyes a friend and a "monument to human simplicity" (*FA*, 11). Nina's fondness of John is the most detailed and dramatized instance in the novel of her generous nature which seeks to help everyone. Her helping John has its comic moments. She inadvertently gives John's landlady romantic notions about him and conversely, as an overzealous chaperone cools John's developing passion for Lydia. John's close friendship with Nina is natural enough given his assignment to make the Arenkoffs comfortable in Dorchester, and given his artistic temperament and aspirations.

The characters and their relationships in *Angels* are too numerous and involved to fully consider here. There is the triangular mock-adulterous love and friendship of Nina and John which retains Val in the wings as a friend and counselor; John's physical attraction for Lydia and his farcical romantic link with his landlady, Mrs. Bliss; Nina's love for her first husband and for Val, and her "romance" with Ganson; the liaisons of Leona Schrantz with George Doore and George Works; Lydia's happy pursuit of Hugo McDonald; Julie Rale's blind love for George Doore; the caretaker marriage of the pitiful Mr. and Mrs. Wattleman—all of these characters, although rendered satirically, work to the conclusion that Horgan develops more tragically in his next novel, *No Quarter Given*: the artist must turn the materials of his own experience, his loves and life, into his own unique art.

No Quarter Given. In 1964 Horgan listed *No Quarter Given* (1935), among his own novels, one of his two favorites—along with *Far From Cibola* (1938).[12] *No Quarter* is an example of Horgan's use of analogous form, because in hearing the autobiography of the central character, composer Edmund Abbey, one also hears echoes of the symphony which he completes just before his death. Abbey's present life in Santa Fe and in Albuquerque is juxtaposed with his past life as a young man and artist in the East by association with his music. The length of the novel (almost 600 pages) and the numerous flashbacks and shifts in locale make it one of Horgan's most complex works of fiction.

Readers and reviewers directed most of their considerations to these structural and stylistic aspects of the novel. Witter Bynner praised Horgan's achievement in terms of the expressiveness of his prose and the humanness of his characters.[13] Helen MacAfee regretted that an analogy between music and fiction was used in writing the novel.[14] Mary McCarthy found the novel formless and inconclusive and the method too oblique for the "novel to impinge on the reader with that poignant sense of reality which its author intends it to have."[15] Other reviewers in America and England saw a lack of unity and found Horgan's style mannered and melodramatic. Seán O'Faoláin, however, found similarities between Horgan's novel and Dreiser's *The Genius* and judged the final result a rare thing of "speed without loss of depth, . . . [with] a pleasing contrapuntal effect, . . . which gives variety to the entire mood."[16]

No Quarter is a more unified and significant novel than many early reviewers perceived. It is the story of Edmund Abbey's life revealed from two perspectives: his past, from childhood into adulthood told by Abbey himself; and his present, told in third person, as he attempts to recover from tuberculosis and compose music. Abbey's past and present lives illustrate his devotion to his art, how an artist experiences growing up, how difficult it is to find and keep the right conditions to encourage his art—and show his refusal to give any quarter, to yield to interferences, even illness. Moreover, his past and present lives converge in his death at the novel's close in a way that goes toward making his death, as was the case with his life, "artistic," for his death song is of his own making. In his physical destruction is also the completion and release of the symphony he struggled so long to realize. Within these two "plots" are interwoven other lives, other biographies, as they are affected by Abbey and as they affect him. They are the lives of artists, of humanity, and its necessity for beauty and love.

As the novel opens, Abbey finds himself stricken with tuberculosis and living in the Santa Fe house of his wife, Georgia, a wealthy and beautiful but frivolous socialite. Three years before, Abbey had met Georgia Barham (recently divorced from her second husband), at the time of the modest success in New York of Abbey's first symphony. Her wealth offered him patronage, and they married—honeymooning in Mexico before Abbey's illness and residence in Santa Fe. Georgia's seventeen-year-old son, David Barham (a youth very much in need of finding himself and a real home), comes from school to visit Edmund and begins to know him as a friend and respect him as an artist. A rivalry develops, unintended on Edmund's part but selfishly sensed by Georgia, for David's allegiance.

David's entry into Edmund's sphere of influence is encouraged by his meeting Maggie Michaelis, a prominent actress who has moved to Santa Fe to heal herself emotionally from disillusionment with her profession and from a broken love affair with a married man. As a means to this she has taken up sculpting. After a chance encounter with Maggie in a Santa Fe church, where they befriend an old Hispanic lady, Concepcion Fuentes, David introduces Maggie to Edmund. All three develop a close friendship centered around the humanist values of art. Complications arise when David falls in love with Maggie only to learn that Maggie and Edmund are in love and that Maggie is his mistress.

The tensions of the plot of the "present" focus on Edmund's developing need to separate from Georgia and marry Maggie and establish a new life for himself and his art. Soon after he divorces Georgia and marries Maggie, Edmund dies but not without a certain triumph—for he has been with Maggie and has completed an important symphony. Rejected by Maggie's love for Edmund but choosing Edmund's way of life as an artist as the truer way than his mother's, David comes into a mature if somewhat lonely self-reliance.

David and Maggie are not so much restored to each other upon Edmund's death, when they see Edmund immortalized in the performance of his work by the famed conductor out of Edmund's past, Angelini, as they are restored to faith in art and its process. Maggie resolves to return to her career as an actress and David is dedicated finally to the ambition he has had for a long time—to become a writer. The end of Edmund's life, as represented by the performance of his music, and listened to with love and pride by Maggie and David, is but a beginning, and Edmund's values are reflected in David's consciousness: "David's exhilaration grew and grew; and he conceived of himself as being full of strength; in a sense, and by their lesson as he could learn it, the heir of those human utterances out of the past which never die."[17]

If the plot of the novel's present works toward the union of Edmund and Maggie and David, and their separation from Georgia's more superficial world of gossip and recrimination, the plot of the novel's past—Edmund's autobiography—works toward the union of Edmund with other artists and lovers, and his separation from them for the sake of his art. Horgan's use of East/West settings reinforces this dynamic. Edmund's realization of his ideals with Maggie in the culture and climate of New Mexico is a culmination to what he had sought and what had only been intimated in the Ganson School of Music in Dorchester and the musical theaters of the East. Ironically, however, in finding his best life and his best work in the West, Edmund also loses himself to illness and disease. The glory of the successful failure that is Edmund's life is that he persevered in uniting his past and his present, his Eastern youth and exploration with his Western maturity and death. His passage from youth to maturity to death is reinforced by the East, West, East cycle of place.

Ultimately, it is impossible to separate the novel's present (that is, Abbey's biography) from the novel's past (that is, Abbey's autobiography). During the course of the novel they merge into one. Furthermore, David's biography, as it is revealed in friendship and identification with Edmund, merges with Edmund's biography. And so does Maggie's life as an actress which the reader hears in chapter 7 (first published as "Slow Curtain" in *Harpers*, February 1935). Other lives, all presented as "biographies" of their own, also merge with Edmund's past life: Carol "Cleopatra" Dean, the flirtatious student at the Ganson School of Music; Bertha Brewer, a doctor's daughter who is Edmund's first love; Sally Warner, his neighbor who helps him find work at the Luxor Theater; Lily Remusat, the famous and temperamental opera singer who hires Edmund as her accompaniest and introduces him to Eduardo Angelini; Peter Fremont, friend and writer; Edmund's surgeon father, Dr. Abbey, who shows his son the meaning of courage in a crisis.

And still others merge with his New Mexico present: Mrs. Mannering, whose life as a pioneer wife Edmund sees in grandly eloquent old age; Concepcion Fuentes and her family, representative of the old and the new Hispanic New Mexican; the Pueblo Indians whose dances become a climactic part of Edmund's life and music; the painter Lucian Roland who leaves his sad and hysterical wife, Bonny, for Georgia. All of these lives merge into Edmund's life and music—that is, the novel.

***Main Line West* and *A Lamp on the Plains*.** In his third and fourth published novels, *Main Line West* (1936) and *A Lamp on the Plains* (1937), Horgan turned from the refined lives of Eastern artists, whether in New York or exiled in the social and real deserts of New Mexico, to deal less satirically, almost naturalistically, with the hard times and tragedies of rootless, unsophisticated people seeking home and community on the plains of the Southwest. Beginning with these two novels, including *Far from Cibola* (1938) and continuing through *The Common Heart* (1942), his last novel before he entered the army and service at the Pentagon during the war, Horgan rendered in art the kinds of insights into people and place that he had made in his own life in New Mexico before and after the family tragedy of his father's death from tuberculosis. He returned to these plains people and their troubles again long after the war in such novels as *Whitewater* (1970) and *The Thin Mountain Air* (1977). Throughout, as his fictive counterparts Edmund Abbey and later "Richard," he developed the keenest of abilities to turn his own experience into poignantly realistic and "moral" fiction—novels that revealed that faith in man and God, though hard won, is essential. In all, Horgan's novels about plains people have earned him preeminence as a writer about Anglo-American settlement in the modern

Southwest in ways that tend to both typify and transcend time and place.

In keeping with Horgan's interest in biography and the novel of maturation, *Main Line West* and *A Lamp on the Plains* feature the life story of Danny Milford. Danny's troubles are many as he tries to shape a future for himself out of a tragic present and past that knows desertion by his father, the hysteria of mob violence, and the death of his mother that leaves him an orphan at the age of thirteen. His struggle is to survive, to keep himself from despair and death of the spirit, to continue to affirm the goodness of life in the face of its cruelty. This is the most important moral issue he faces.

In this effort he is not without his benefactors. There is his mother, evangelist Irma Milford, who through her desperate love and insistence on goodness gives him direction. There is the mechanic, Newt Jimson, who wants more for Danny than he ever had. There is the preposterous embezzler, professor, and humanist, W. Winston Burlington, who lights Danny's quest for knowledge through reading and study. There is the rancher Wade McGraw who adopts Danny and treats him like one of his own children—placing him in a military school with his sons that offers him a chance for education and a decent future. And most of all, there is in him the blood of his vagabond parents that makes up his own essential character. Among a motley cast of plains people Danny succeeds in his life struggle to stay true to his mother's best hope and the inheritance of his character. The conclusion of *A Lamp on the Plains* leaves him strong and sound at the age of sixteen, on the threshold of a maturity that should see him through.

For its brief length of 200 pages, *Main Line West* moves far and fast, following several stages and influences in the lives of father, mother, and son through several Southwestern places at the time of World War I. Across Kansas, Colorado, New Mexico, Texas, Arizona, and California, the saga of the Milfords unfolds. The railroad, the main line West, serves as a literal means of travel and a unifying image of their wanderings. Divided into five books entitled succinctly "The Father," "The Mother," "The Spirit," "The Power," and "The Son," the story profiles each of these characters and qualities.

Kansas is the starting point of Horgan's story—the place where traveling salesman Daniel Milford, on the road between Athens and Freola, stops one evening at the farmhouse of Shide Kinneyman and meets Mrs. Kinneyman's sister, Irma Gruvers. It is the meeting of opposites: the pious Irma, the austere Kinneymans, the worldly Daniel. Out of the mismatched union of Daniel and Irma comes Danny Milford, Jr. As soon as Dan learns of Irma's pregnancy and realizes that it means the ruination of his mobility he prepares to desert them. He buys a café in California and then leaves.

Born in California, Danny spends his childhood there in the company of the café's Chinese cook, K'ang-Hsui, and the town doctor's son, Tom McBridge. Irma, resolved to make it on her own for Danny's sake, saves what money she can and plans a return to Kansas. She confers in longing and still loving conversation with her departed husband about her and Danny's future, and turning back to her earlier religious life is "called" to become an evangelist, preaching a message of love and peace. It is a message made all the stronger by the word she receives of her estranged husband's death in the war. But it is a message that the wartime patriots increasingly do not want to hear—not even from the leading lady evangelist in the West.

After selling the café and traveling over a half-dozen states preaching the word, the message backfires and peace becomes violence as she and Danny are stoned in a small town called Los Algodones. On the main line west out of town at night, protected as much as possible by Danny, Irma dies. She is buried in Driscoll, Arizona, and with only sixteen dollars and much sorrow Danny hops a train headed East into an unknown future, a future that begins with the opening of *A Lamp on the Plains* when Danny again finds himself in New Mexico, in a small southeastern plains town close to Roswell, called Vrain.

Vrain "was such a town as drew its very character off the land where it stood; its character in stuffs; in occupations; and in people."[18] Danny is destined to draw strength from the best that is in that place and those people but not to settle there permanently. At its worst there is much in Vrain that is petty and backward. It is not the lamp on the plains to which the title and the central metaphor of the novel refer. In part, the railroad is a lamp because it leads away to the larger world. It is in the reading room of the Santa Fe Railroad under the tutelage of one of Danny's more "disreputable" rescuers, Professor W. W. Burlington, that the lamp of civility begins to shine for Danny:

> It was ugly and barren and merely a shelter; but if anyone wanted to use it so, it was a shelter not only for the body, but also the mind; and

the light was so limited into little areas of glow from each lamp on its table that nothing need be visible but the place of the reader's thought, where he might walk far, and for so long, that he would grow, while that journey lasted. (*LP*, 101)

Horgan emphasizes that any lamp shining on the desolation of the plains is welcome and significant, and there are several in the novel.

The home, be it ever so sanctimonious, of another of Danny's benefactors, the Reverend and Mrs. Robert Hopeman, is another lamp which lights Danny's way. Hopeman, as his name indicates, extends a double hope for the congregation of Vrain: "The blessings of God and the nourishments of culture" (*LP*, 85). But the "lamps" of Hopeman's spiritual guidance and Burlington's railroad library, his lectures and recitations, come to oppose each other. Burlington's refined ways with the ladies in his reading club are too much for the jealousies of the town husbands, including Sheriff Hardy Cleade and the Reverend Hopeman—and for Newt Jimson, a rival of the professor's for the attention of the waitresses, Myrtle and Earlene. Hopeman's and Burlington's conflicting moral values lead to the professor's being thrown in jail and Danny's helping him break out and leave town on the train. Danny thus becomes a lamp of friendship.

In the second half of the novel Danny is taken out of jail, where he is held for his part in the professor's escape, by Wade McGraw and put to work on his ranch in nearby Cedar. The Cedar ranch and what Danny experiences there in the love and friendship of McGraw's daughter, Kathleen, serves as another "lamp" on the plains for Danny. Likewise, the military school in Roswell where McGraw sends his sons, Henry and Stephen, becomes the brightest plains life-lamp for Danny. The McGraw family and ranch at Cedar and the military school at Roswell, in spite of the hazing by Stephen McGraw, offer Danny a much improved life than he knows in Vrain.

His third and fourth published novels, *Main Line West* and *A Lamp On the Plains*, established Horgan in the minds of readers as an author who knew the plains people of the Southwest as well as the artists of the East. Character and setting, people and place gained most attention in both novels. The towns themselves seemed to assume the magnitude of characters for more than one reviewer. Vrain, said Edith Mirrielees is "vigorously and continuously alive," and New Mexico was the force dominating the book: "In his portrayal of the Southwest at work upon its residents the author is at his best."[19] Alfred Carter chose to read *Main Line West* as a small town novel: "It is . . . a statement of the conditions under which the western character of modern time lives in a pattern of small town and western city."[20] Margaret Wallace wondered whether or not Horgan would continue Danny Milford's story into maturity.[21] In significant ways, *Whitewater*, published thirty-odd years later, becomes just that sequel.

Far From Cibola* and *The Common Heart. As favorites go, Horgan regards *Far From Cibola* (1938) the one novel among his many which best satisfies the artist's problem of "the solution of form."[22] After making several wash drawings of some of the people who congregated in Roswell in the depressed 1930s, Horgan tells how the novel almost came to write itself: "I wrote *Far From Cibola* in twelve consecutive days of entire possession by its form and its echo of the passionate effects of human lives upon each other when all desires have a common object."[23] That form and its outlines make for the most beautiful literary experience among Horgan's prewar novels.

Far From Cibola follows the passing of one April day in 1933 from morning through afternoon into evening, moving from the outskirts of town to downtown and back to the surrounding plains in an odelike movement. Individual characters are introduced first and as the sun arcs out the day these plains people are drawn to a mid-morning meeting at the courthouse, to a highschool track meet, to everyday town business. Desires grow, needs focus, competition and self-interest merge into mob hysteria which is defused by a tragic accident: a youth, Franz Vosz, is shot by the sheriff's warning bullets into a tree where the boy happens to be perched. The crowd disperses. Apologies are made. Life goes on—continuing its cycle like the passing of the sun and the seasons. In his afterword to the novel, Horgan says the underlying theme is human charity. And it is seen, in keeping with the polarities in the novel, in its presence and its absence. Some of the characters are more charitable than others, closer to the mythical, sought-after golden city of Cibola.

The distance implicit in Horgan's title is significant and the metaphorical ramifications of the hunting, finding and missing of Cibola are multifold. Although the nexus of activity, the "X" marking the "treasure" of federal relief, is the town courthouse, there are other Cibolas dramatized in the novel. The one certainty of Cibola is its elusiveness, always shimmering between fantasy and fact.

On the periphery, in the opening chapter, are Ellen Rood and her two children facing a larger crisis of a dead father and husband, poverty—and the smaller yet symbolic crisis of killing a rattlesnake near the chicken house. Like another widow with a chickenhouse inheritance, Willa Shoemaker, in *The Common Heart* (1942), Ellen Rood courageously protects her own in the face of the various crosses and crucifixions that are her life. (Hers is one of many symbolic names in the novel.) Her act of confronting the evil embodied in the snake's threatening presence, of killing the snake, is its own legacy—just as Irma Milford's courage is for her son, Danny.

The Rood family is a society which establishes an ideal of self-reliance against which the larger family of plains people, and beyond them the national family, the "government" is reflected. Ellen Rood's courage, Horgan suggests, will last far into the future. In the "picture" of the opening incident of Cibola is the significance of the novel. As is characteristic in Horgan's fiction, the elements of nature as they are known in the climate of the plains—their special forms of dust and wind, drought and rain, heat and cold—are emblematic of life and death, humanity's dust to dust migration. The impending accidental death of Franz Vosz is anticipated in the opening chapter. Ellen's battle with the snake is a hot and dusty one and her "original sin" as well as her courage suggested in the confrontation is proven later in the day at the courthouse gathering.

The evil in man, his lack of charity as well as his redemption through love is to be proved many times that day. The snake will not die until sundown and in that course of time Franz Vosz will be dead and so will the tubercular vagabond, Leo, who dies cold and alone in a junk car. Surrounding Ellen's life struggle is the land and the legend of Cibola.

If Ellen Rood is associated with Christ and the quests of the Conquistadors, old Andrew Lark, in the simple act of greasing his windmill, offers another "picture" of stamina and lust for life, of money brought West and spent, of many extremes of winter and summer on the plains. He is his own legend, his own Conquistador.

As Andrew's wife Nona watches fearfully and scolds him to come down, he climbs to the top of the windmill "as if he had gone on a far journey." It is a prideful climb filled with the capriciousness, the "lark" of the moment—a scene that is balanced ironically later in the day with Franz Vosz's capricious climb up a cottonwood tree to get a better view of the activity outside the courthouse. Like Billy

Breedlove's climb up the Belvedere water tower in *Whitewater*, Vosz's climb and his fall with a bullet in his chest—and his ride home to the family farm—is a journey to death. That night, after being in the crowd, witnessing the youth's and the town's tragedy, and being at the Vosz home so filled with mourning, Lark dozes in his chair alive with a sense of luck. As Lark gets safely into bed for yet another night, the well-greased windmill and the wind acting idly upon it become a metaphor for his entire life's striving: "He nodded his head with satisfaction when all he could hear was a constant airy w'anging from the metal blades that turned slowly, and the metal fin that strove always to be parallel with the wind" (*MS*, 262).

While Andrew Lark sleeps in warmth and satisfaction, and others of the town meet the night in their own comfort-searching ways, Leo leaves his rideless road, dreams of California successes, and finds shelter in a burned-out car—stationary and cold in a roadside field. Rejected as a panhandler at Fat's Cafe, Leo's journey, his climb and fall, are both meager and final. Unable to climb the barbed wire fence he falls and rolls under it, crawling to the wrecked car. Once inside the car the wind plays on the surrounding junk much differently than it does on Lark's maintained windmill. Isolated and dead, Leo "lay in his car, in some way a responsibility of all the lives he had ever known" (*MS*, 276). On the New Mexico plains he is far from the promised lands of California and Cibola.

Given the odelike form of *Cibola*, each incident, each person and group of persons affects the other. The center is reflected in the periphery, the opening in the closing. Thus, Andrew Lark in his bed listening to the wind and the sound of a successful climb and Leo dozing off to death in his junked car, suggest the journeys made to town and away from town, all implied in the title: the legendary journey of the Spaniards north toward the golden cities of Cibola and the journey of the sun by day and century across the plains.

The Vosz family is at the center of the day's events. Of her three fine sons—Richard, Joseph, and Franz—Franz is the favorite. Everything comes easy for Franz, a natural athlete and runner. In his zest for living and with crowds of admirers, he is very much like Billy Breedlove who also dies just before leading his high school track team to victory. It is because of Mrs. Vosz's whimpering insistence that Franz goes to town that morning with his parents rather than practice for the afternoon track meet like his brothers. His mother's wish is the ironic first cause of his ensuing death. But it is only one of many ironic choices: Franz's deciding to climb the tree; the sheriff drawing his gun to fire three random shots into the tree and hitting the "fresh leaves" and the young flesh of Vosz.

In Horgan's handling of the shooting of Franz Vosz are shadows of Ellen Rood's early morning encounter with the snake. Through associated descriptions, the snake episode is brought to mind and so is the tree in Eden. Mortality. Dust. Franz falls from the tree into the dust. And on the ride home, accompanied too by Mrs. Rood, a stirred cloud of dust darkens the way and, in association with the morning rattlesnake and the serpent of Eden, "rattled faintly upon the faded surface of the car" (*MS*, 246).

Heart DeLancy (who does much to incite the crowd action against the government relief workers and the sheriff at the courthouse) and her lover, Rolf Kunkel, pick up Richard and Joe Vosz at the track meet—where other pistol shots for other purposes ring out in ironic innocence. They drive to the Vosz farm facing the same dust and death. Imagistically, Horgan blends the plains with its people, natural landscape with the landscape of the mind.

At this juncture the novel changes to evening. Young Donald Rood takes one last look at the snake which twitches finally and forever at sundown. Ellen is back with her children, vaguely certain that "someone was responsible for her, and must help her, must help everyone in difficulty (*MS*, 252).

Few reviewers sufficiently appreciated the organic form of *Cibola.* Robert Van Gelder said, though some readers may see a triumph of composition, "to the majority it will seem formless."[24] Otis Ferguson concluded, "It is a minor work beside *A Lamp on the Plains.*"[25] Dorothy Hughes found Horgan too dispassionate and distanced for a subject she termed "social chaos."[26]

The Common Heart (1942), Horgan's last novel before his duty during World War II, is a family biography of Dr. Peter Rush and his wife Susan (Noonie) Larkin and their residence in Albuquerque during the 1920s. The present of the novel is only a few months—from winter through summer—during one year. It is a crisis year, however, in their marriage, threatened by Susan's illness and the appearance of another woman, with whom Dr. Rush falls in love for a time. In this context the past becomes a very important part of the present (and the future) of Peter and Noonie Rush's life. Through numerous interpolated narratives in the manner of *No Quarter Given*, Peter Rush's memories cross into the present: his medical years at Cornell; his internship at St. Luke's hospital in New York; his courtship of Susan—including various fun and crisis times with her family and friends in Rochester and their eventual marriage in 1906. Moreover, a visit to his Colorado cousin, Jack Winterhood, in 1892 when Rush was fifteen is dramatized as an important phase in his life. There are memories about his parents, who like Dr. Rush and his wife combined the East and the West in their marriage, making the comparison between Rush and his thirteen-year-old son, Donald, all the more appropriate.

Because Rush is a physician and a historian with imagination (a character who anticipates Howard Debler in *Mexico Bay*), there are also regional "memories" that reach much further into the past of Rush's beloved New Mexico homeland—back to 1850 and a U.S. Cavalry and Navajo skirmish east of Albuquerque; beyond that to General Kearny's 1846 march into Santa Fe and Albuquerque; and even beyond that to Christmas day 1598 some twenty miles north of Albuquerque as spent by Captain José Diego de Nájera, one of Oñate's soldiers and the father of "the first child among the new settlers who colonized New Mexico that year" (*MS*, 419). Through such memories and histories the common heart of the plains people and larger humanity is affirmed by Dr. Rush. Each interpolated memory and narrative reinforces the recurrent frontier faced by everyman.

Understanding Rush's character, his love of humanity and of New Mexico history, and how he comes to a stronger heart in his marriage is fundamental to reconciling the other moral issues in the novel. These cluster around the friendship of the doctor's son, Donald, and Wayne Shoemaker as they awaken to responsibilities beyond adolescence, class distinctions, and money; and the work at the Harvey House of Wayne's widowed and loving mother, Willa Shoemaker, and her dreams of selling her husband's chicken-ranch legacy and returning home to Albion, Michigan, to show her old friends that she did become somebody after all. Of related involvement is the ripening romantic infatuation of Willa's daughter, Martha, and the young doctor-to-be Richmond (Bun) Summerfield. And finally, there is the impatient Hispanic grandfather, Don Hilario Ascarete as he readies himself for death. All of these biographies and relationships touch on Dr. Rush's life and his need as a physician of body, mind, and spirit to minister to the common heart of man.

As the novel opens, Dr. Rush's marriage is less than ideal. What began as a strong marriage fourteen years ago in Rochester now finds

Noonie a semi-invalid, reluctant to any thought of more children ever since Donald's birth. She is despondent and confines herself to reading frivolous magazines in the bedroom of the comfortable, servant-attended Rush home. Dr. Rush can do nothing to change the situation and the implication is that Noonie's malaise, her lack of heart, is an illness within her deepest self. Dr. Rush has his work and his interest in books about local history, and he combines the two by driving around Albuquerque and vicinity and finding the exact places he reads about. At other times he is visiting patients or in the operating room at St. Joseph's hospital.

Noonie yearns for the East but it was long ago decided that she would go where her husband took her when he finished medical school—back to his home in Albuquerque. Donald senses that something is wrong at home, and Dr. Rush comes to realize this in a new way. Donald prefers to spend most of his time, when he is not exploring the town and the river on his bicycle, in the poor but hospitable Shoemaker house. The main burden of the novel, then, entails the healing of Noonie and the restoration of family harmony in the Rush household.

A three-way moral crisis brings this restoration about—three related crises in each of the lives of the Rush family. For Peter Rush it takes the form of a patient from the East, Mrs. Carmichael Foster, who has come to Albuquerque for her health. It turns out that she is a noted novelist. Rush and Molly Foster fall in love but he realizes that his duty is to Noonie and Donald. Noonie is driven to try to kill herself by taking too much medication; but she is found and revived by Dr. Rush. In a miraculous metamorphosis, she recovers to a new love of life and her husband so that by the novel's end she awaits the birth of another child. As for Donald, he expiates his guilt for shooting out all the windows in Willa Shoemaker's chicken ranch by throwing his birthday .22-caliber rifle into the Rio Grande—and through an unspoken forgiveness communicated to him by his father. Molly Foster makes her moral choice by leaving Albuquerque and by remaining loyal to her art which amounts to a thanksgiving for life. She tells Rush: "To sing a song, or to tell a tale and so somehow tap that universal thing in the response of other people—this is about as close to giving thanks as an artist can ever come" (*MS*, 402). Horgan's novels about plains people amount to just that, thanks for the common heart of humanity.

Reviewers, again, failed to wholly appreciate *The Common Heart.*

William DuBois said Horgan "has outlined a series of apparently related crises that should add up to a novel, and don't."[27] Stanley Vestal felt Horgan's characters "adolescents and shallow women," inferior to the New Mexico setting.[28] Diana Trilling responded perceptively, saying, "This is a novel that argues for love."[29]

Horgan's novels about plains people have attracted the most attention from critics. Several specialists in Western American literature have offered their insights—all, for the most part, incisive. John R. Milton describes the characters in these novels as "small, unheroic except as the little people of the earth are heroic in their survival and their occasional small victories over mundane problems; but Horgan's method is to illuminate them, including the shadows of despair, hopelessness, and tragedy, so that they stand etched as in a portrait."[30] The "portrait" is really a mural reaching not only across the plains of the Southwest but across all of America.

The Habit of Empire. *The Habit of Empire*, (1939), one of Horgan's two historical novels, deals not with Anglo-American settlement on the modern plains of the Southwest but with Hispanic colonization of New Mexico and the impact of that coming on sixteenth-century Native Americans. In one sense, Horgan's portraiture of Juan de Oñate in this novel is an extension of his first book, *Men of Arms* (1931), and an anticipation of his other historical novel, *A Distant Trumpet* (1960), about Indian wars in Arizona and Mexico three hundred years after Oñate's conflicts of colonization.[31] Thus *Empire* is a significant novel on several grounds: (1) as an adaptation of historical source materials; (2) for its portrayals of Hispanics and Native Americans; and (3) for the place it occupies in relation to Horgan's other "military" writings.

In *Empire* Horgan gives an account of Oñate's expedition into New Mexico in 1598 which climaxed in the battle of Acoma in January 1599. It was an expedition intended for King Philip II, an imperial settlement which included as part of its plan the conversion of the Pueblo Indians to Christianity. Other men of arms than Oñate made the expedition what it was and Horgan follows their course as well: Oñate's nephews, Juan de Zaldivar and his brother Don Vicente; Father Alonzo de Martinez, a Franciscan; Oñate's notary, Bocanegra; the Acoma chief, Zutucapan—and most importantly, Captain Gaspar Perez de Villagrá, Oñate's valiant procurer general, a soldier, historian, poet. Horgan bases his fictionalized *Empire* on Villagrá's eye-witness acount, written in thirty-four cantos of epic verse and entitled the *History of New Mexico.*

A prototype for Horgan's humanist men of arms like his composite General Crook-Quait in *Trumpet*, Villagrá too loves Virgil and stalwart soldiers like Aeneas, as evidenced in the opening stanza of his history: "Of arms I sing, and of that heroic son. / Of his wondrous deeds and of his victories won."[32] Horgan, in adapting Villagrá's persona and "song" to his own purposes of the historical novel obliterates Villagrá's mock humility and elevates him to an equal level of heroism with Oñate and the Zaldivar brothers.

Horgan is sensitive to the problems inherent in dealing with brutality and bloodshed on the side of both the Spanish and the Pueblo Indians at the Acoma battle. Always one to acknowledge, as a Christian humanist, the best and the worst sides of man, Horgan seeks to get at the psychology of Spanish empire building not so much to glorify or even justify it as to understand it: "Conquest and warfare were conmmonplaces, instruments of policy and weapons of faith. Such means were cruel, and later ages have seen the need for outlawing them, and will so prevail. But in their time, no other arm of effect was available in society."[33] To say that cruel means were seen by the sixteenth-century Spanish as justifying their ends is not to say that Horgan justifies them. This book suggests that in spite of itself, history like fiction is never really "objective" and to sense the Spanish "habit of empire" in Horgan's telling of the bloodshed at Acoma is not to match up too closely Villagrá's persona with Horgan's.

At the time of publication there were some sensibilities that clearly equated persona and author and cheered the gallant Spanish over the "barbarous" Indians, hailing the slaughter at Acoma as a Spanish success. Others viewed Horgan as too much taken with a one-sided, "wave-of-the-future interpretation of history."[34]

Considered forty years after publication in an era of keen sensibility to issues of civil and human rights for Native Americans, Horgan says he would not revise the book but let it stand—with perhaps a special foreword,

> to call attention again, which is quite implicit in the text, to the fact that the conflict between the Spaniards and the Indians is a matter of history; and that the Indians were defeated and barbarically treated by the Spaniards also belongs to historical truth. And finally that the account is es-

sentially a fictional effort in that I have taken the epic poem of Captain Villagrá . . . and given it whatever imaginative extravagance it seemed to me the violent story required. (H-2)

Horgan's "imaginative extravagance" is more abbreviated but almost as lyrical as Villagrá's account.

The central episode of *Empire*, the full Spanish attack on Acoma, derives from the death of Juan Zaldivar and the revenge of his brother and Oñate. On 22 December 1598 Father de Martinez conducts a requiem High Mass for Juan Zaldivar and the ten other victims of the first battle one month earlier. Vicente is seen filled with a sense of honor and the desire for revenge. Oñate is more deliberate, caught up in remorse and "fearless within the standards of his own character" but calmly seeking advice of Father de Martinez in the matter. The priest argues that the Acomas must be put down, but not out of vengeance: "Indians must be slain to make them respect the reign of Christ and King" (*HE*, 74). So the two issues Oñate must consider are vengeance as advocated by Vicente and respect for authority as "reasoned" by Martinez. Both reasons mean death to Indians. In church, kneeling before the altar in an all night vigil of prayer, Oñate seeks his decision before Christ. Deciding to attack, he prays only for success: "A weaker man might have gone to pray in the hope for an inspiration to guide his resolve. General Juan de Oñate decided; and prayed for victory" (*HE*, 76).

The attack comes at dawn on 22 January 1599. The "Storm Toward Heaven," as Horgan entitles the chapter, is difficult for the Spanish and they depend on divine help. Throughout the battle, on various fronts, they call out the name of their saint, "Santiago," Saint James the Great of Compostella, patron of Spain. A chasm 200 feet deep and twelve feet across must be crossed and after a night of preparations it is bridged at dawn of the second day of fighting. To the cry of "Santiago," Zaldivar's preliminary force reaches Acoma. But the log-bridge is removed and used as a battering ram, leaving the main body of soldiers without a way to cross the chasm. Heroic Villagrá jumps the chasm, picks up the log, and again makes a bridge with it, allowing the main force of soldiers access to the pueblo. The sound of war drums versus the name of Santiago are heard throughout three days of fighting. A second request for surrender is not heeded and the serpentin is moved into position to destroy the entire pueblo, dwelling by dwelling.

The Indians are rendered noble in their surrender. The old men come forward and ask for mercy. Zutucapan is dead and the surviving chief, Chumpo, can only marvel—as can the Spaniards—at the vision of Santiago which led the Spaniards from the clouds during the battle.

In an epilogue, Horgan recounts the visit to Acoma of Father Juan Ramirez thirty years later in 1629. The city is rebuilt. But hatred remains and when Father Ramirez ascends the trail to the pueblo he is met by a shower of arrows. Armed only with his prayers to God and his crucifix which he holds up for protection, the arrows miraculously do not touch him. It is proof that Oñate's "habit of empire" has prevailed over the Indians.

Postwar Novels

Horgan's most renowned postwar writings are his two Pulitzer-prize winning histories, *Great River* (1954) and *Lamy of Santa Fe* (1975). But the novelistic products of what might be considered his second start as a writer, after the dispiriting four years between 1942 and 1946, evidence both a return to the themes, characters, and settings of his beginnings as a novelist during the 1930s, and a mature advancement—a refinement of former realistic-satirical techniques, and the achievement of even more beautiful creations. Two works of his second phase as a novelist take World War II as their subject: *Give Me Possession* (1957) and *Memories of the Future* (1966). As novels about soldiers and society they invite comparison with *A Distant Trumpet* (1960). Thus his seven prewar novels are balanced, in the early 1980s, with eight other novels which establish as his best novels the Richard trilogy, published over a period of thirteen years between 1964 and 1977, *Whitewater* (1970), *Mexico Bay* (1982), and *Trumpet* (along with *Far From Cibola* published in his prewar period), and secure for him a place as an American novelist who has—in the face of changing styles and postmodernist innovations—survived and, more impressively, succeeded in his allegiance to the realistic tradition. This accomplishment is all the more noteworthy when seen in the light of his career not just as a novelist of fifty years standing, but as a versatile man of letters, with both quality short fiction and nonfiction to his credit.

A Distant Trumpet. *A Distant Trumpet* (1960) is the best known and best received of Horgan's "military" novels. Started as early as 1946, parts of what became the finished novel appeared throughout the 1950s in *Colliers* and the *Saturday Evening Post*. Concerned not with world wars I and II but the Civil War and Apache wars of the 1880s, *Trumpet*, like Horgan's other military novels, combines comedy, realism, and American history. Horgan's works on Abraham Lincoln also are reflected in the novel.

In his dedication to *Trumpet* Horgan alludes to a "family anecdote" told him at the time of his leaving the service in 1946.[35] The story he heard concerned a bride taken to a remote cavalry post in Arizona a century ago and her insistence on bringing with her a set of Waterford crystal glassware which survived the journey only to be dropped upon arrival at the sight of the first Apache who, as it turned out, was a scout at the post. Over ten years that incident burgeoned into a historical novel that follows several interconnecting lives over several generations and across a continent.

Reception was mixed. Frederick H. Guidry termed it "highly readable, broadly informative, and consciously inspirational," and "above the level of a run-of-the-fort adventure story."[36] Paul Engle judged the book "the finest novel yet on the Southwest in its setting."[37] Other novelists agreed. Dorothy M. Johnson termed it "big, tense, vivid, exciting."[38] And Mari Sandoz wrote, "What lifts the book above the usual frontier post romance is the author's feeling for the region and its people."[39] Other reviewers were less than pleased. *Booklist* said, "An overdose of sentimentality and the stereotyping of some characters somewhat weaken the story."[40] The *New Yorker* called it "A likely adventure story swollen by irrelevant material into something quite grandiose and tedious."[41] A British assessment suggested the novel could only be popular in America.[42]

The novel did well in America with almost 600,000 hardcover copies in print by 1967 and six paperback editions by 1970. The movie version was judged a failure. Directed by Raoul Walsh and starring Troy Donahue and Suzanne Pleshette, the film was released by Warner Brothers in 1964. When the movie finally appeared in Horgan's neighborhood theater in Connecticut, he avoided it, saying, "If it is good . . . then I deserve no credit. If it is bad, then I deserve no blame."[43] Judith Crist typified critics' reception of the movie: "Any resemblance between movie and novel is largely the coincidence of names and places. . . . There is only one Esperanto subtitle fitting. . . . It is 'ugh.' "[44]

James Day mistakenly calls *Trumpet* "Horgan's only effort in the area of the historical novel," but praises it as "an excellent historical novel."[45] William T. Pilkington thinks *Trumpet* "far above average as a historical novel" but disappointingly "contrived and, worse, stereotyped."[46] Such concerns establish a context for considering the novel.

The two great historical happenings which serve as dramatic backdrops for *Trumpet* are the disruptions of the Civil War and the settling of the West. With the use of multiple narrators, Horgan recreates the nostalgia and promise which the war and the West held for several men of arms—U.S. Cavalry and Apache—at remote Fort Delivery in Arizona Territory during the 1880s. The overriding design of the novel is biographical: through flashbacks the life story of each of the characters is given, particularly as shaped during the Civil War. As part of the design, the life-story of one of the central characters, General Alexander Quait, is told. The theme is likewise biographical in that the novel advances the notion that human character in large and small ways shapes historical events. A "memories of the future" motif is at work in this novel as well—particularly in the character of one of the soldier heroes, Matthew Carlton Hazard, whose military career is followed in the major plot line.

The novel begins in a seemingly disconnected way with Hazard looking back to happier times—before, because of his own sense of honor, he refuses to accept the Congressional Medal of Honor and resigns from the Army. He tells a vague group of listeners identified as "they," presumably his family, that he remembers knowing his future before it happened. The earliest thing he knew was who he was and who he was going to be. The novel is the telling of that story. It is both a suspenseful and a known opening for the novel and one that has within it the entire structure of the book as biography after biography is recounted and related to Matthew's own life-telling which is the novel.

In keeping with the nature of *Trumpet* as both novel and history, Matthew is both individual and typical, fictive character and representative of real Arizona Indian fighters in the history of the West—just as Abraham Lincoln and the other presidents in the novel are both personages in history and personages in story. As so often with his fiction, it is both tempting and futile to match up real people and historical situations with Horgan's versions of them. Even his Lincoln as true historical personage is still Horgan's rendering of his own perception of "Father Abraham." And the eccentric, scholarly General

Quait who dominates the novel, both is and is not the legendary General George F. Crook. (Horgan's portrayal of Quait mirrors that of Oñate in *Empire*, down to the chewing of the ends of the general's mustache.) The renegade Apache chiefs Rainbow Son and Sebastian are recognizable but fictive approximations of Geronimo and Nachez. So too Lieutenant Hazard is Lieutenant Charles B. Gatewood or Captain Henry W. Lawton only in part. White Horn is and is not a stereotype. The novel's Fort Delivery may or may not be Fort Huachuca or Fort Bowie or one of at least seventy other Arizona frontier forts.

Without tracing precisely where Horgan follows and departs from General Crook's victories over the Chiricahua in the Southwest and finally into the Sierra Madre range of Mexico, the approximations of such an enterprise provide bases for the forward direction of the plot and its climax. As such, the character delineations focus on the moral and military issues involved, the promises and responsibilities incurred in the subjugation of the Apaches by white soldiers and politicians. Complementing this are the moral and social issues surrounding duty and honor among soldiers, officer to officer and officer to his men (Anglo and Native American); among husbands and wives, children and parents, individuals and nation—humanity's responsibility to humanity.

There are many men of arms in *Trumpet*, heroes and cowards of varying degree and kind. When Matthew is only four his father dies at the battle of Chickamauga and he is replaced by Matthew himself and by Abraham Lincoln, the commander in chief who one day in 1864 comes through Matthew's Fox Creek, Indiana, home and makes him a soldier at the age of seven. Stopping his train to find out what Matthew wants as he runs after it, Lincoln tells him, " 'If my father's child can get to be President, your father's child can make his heart's desire' " (*DT*, 19).

To demonstrate his blessing, Lincoln takes a blue cap from a nearby soldier and gives it to the boy, advising him to go to West Point when he grows up. Believing Lincoln's words and keeping the blue soldier cap throughout his life as visible proof of his heart's desire, Matthew does go to West Point; meets and proposes marriage to Laura Greenleaf; is commissioned a second lieutenant of cavalry upon graduation in 1880 and assigned to duty at Fort Delivery in southern Arizona, sixty miles from the Mexican border. On the insistence of Laura's mother, Drusilla Greenleaf, who hopes the separation will lessen her daughter's love, it is agreed that only after one year's service on the Indian frontier would consent be given for Matthew's marriage to Laura. The story then follows Matthew's life at Fort Delivery during that year, his brief return to New York to marry Laura, and their experiences together during another year's duty at Fort Delivery before transfer back to Washington with General Quait—where Hazard refuses the Medal of Honor because his scout, White Horn, is held captive with other Apaches in Florida.

Several soldiers of the heroic stature of his father and of Lincoln affect Matthew's character. They are General Quait who engineers the Apache campaign; White Horn, the Apache scout recruited by Quait as part of a new policy; Major Hiram Hyde Prescott, appointed commander of Fort Delivery after Matthew's arrival; Captain A. Cedric Gray, an Englishman and the fort's surgeon; Private Olin Rainey, the troop trumpeter, and his friend, Private Brian Calahan. More cowardly types who serve as foils to Hazard and truer men of arms are: First Lieutenant Theodore Mainwaring, the fort's acting commanding officer before Prescott's arrival; Captain Adrian Brinker, General Quait's adjutant and Matthew's rival for Laura; Sergeant Blickner and Private Cranshaw whose separate but related desertions break the moral and military laws of soldiering which Hazard upholds.

A Distant Trumpet is a novel of manners as well as a military western, and the lives of several women also affect Hazard. (Whether or not Owen Wister's prototypic East/West, female/male conflicts in *The Virginian* (1902) consciously influenced Horgan in this regard, intriguing parallels can be drawn.) These women are Emma Hazard, his mother; Laura Greenleaf, important first as fiancée and then as wife to Matthew; Laura's mother, Drusilla Godwin Greenleaf, representative of the kind of domineering wife Laura is determined not to be; Kitty Mainwaring, the dissatisfied wife of Ted Mainwaring who seeks recognition in flirtatious and disturbed ways; Jessica Dryden Prescott, an ideal commanding officer's wife—sincere friend and adviser to all; Maud Cantwell Gray, a devoted companion to her surgeon husband.

Even though he is tempted into an adulterous affair by Kitty Mainwaring while engaged to Laura, Hazard's character remains noble. From the moment he meets Lincoln he is destined for success as a soldier and a man. But his character is put to the test inside and outside the fort, socially and militarily. Indeed, his name implies that he must face the risks of his choices. His victory through virtue of character is not a cloistered one. He prepares himself step by step, first in small then in larger ways to pass his greatest test. This comes in a mythical way when he must journey into the Sierra Madre stronghold of Rainbow Son. He goes alone, except for his companion—also an archetypal friend—the scout, White Horn. That journey and Rainbow Son's surrender is the supreme event upon which all of General Quait's strategies rest.

Horgan attempts a humanistic view of the Apaches through his portrayal of White Horn and of General Quait's and Lieutenant Hazard's attitudes and assumptions about him and his people's ways. White Horn exists as two people in the novel, between two worlds and his fate very much affects Hazard's. General Quait and Hazard regard the scout as White Horn, with all the dignity that his true Indian name signifies. Horgan intends the reader to regard White Horn this way too since White Horn's biography of his youth deals largely with the ritual of his naming. It is the disreputable Sergeant Blickner who nicknames him "Joe Dummy" on first meeting. And though White Horn remains honorable as Indian and cavalry scout—notably in his benevolence and friendship for Hazard, his wife and their son, and in his role in the capture of Rainbow Son—it is as Joe Dummy that he is sent to Florida as a guard and interpreter only to be betrayed by Army policy and held captive with all of the Chiricahua. Quait, Hazard, and Prescott view White Horn as an individual entitled to his heritage, as a human who has justified the trust extended to him by General Quait in making him an Army scout.

Some might view the novel as unfairly favoring the Army over the Apache. Assimilation into the Anglo-American culture is assumed inevitable and desirable. Quait and his men kill Indians. So does White Horn. And the Indians kill and mutilate whites.

However, Horgan must be credited with partially humanizing stereotyped accounts of both Anglo-Americans and Native Americans. White Horn, in his "turncoat" role, an Indian in the white man's army fighting against his people, struggles with his good-bad self perceptions. In deciding to accept Quait's argument that he and his people will die unless they reconcile themselves to superior forces and the inevitable white settlement of their land, White Horn is convinced that he can do more for his people's survival as a scout than as a renegade. In his final betrayal and captivity is the irony of going from captive to captive and not to freedom. He has, however, had the true friendship and loyalty of Hazard. It is the same kind of irony reflected in Hazard's honorable refusal of a dishonorable Medal of Honor. And it is that action through which Horgan affirms White Horn's and Hazard's human worth as soldiers.

Give Me Possession* and *Memories of the Future. As novels which follow the biographies of American Army and Navy officers from roughly 1914 to 1946 in the United States, Europe, and the Pacific, *Give Me Possession* (1957) and *Memories of the Future* (1966) complement each other as moral statements—at times through satirical means—of man's striving for civilization and humanity, for good, in the face of mechanized barbarism, inhumanity, and evil. Despite their noble purpose, as war novels they are weakened by sentimentality and cloying portrayals of soldiers and socialites.

Gerald Walker called *Possession* a novel "of manners, mammon, and the Golden Gate."[47] *Library Journal* described it as the story of David Bonbright and "his first acquaintance with a way of life that accepts poverty, illness, and catastrophe as a background to something more than survival, and learns . . . that he cannot return to things as they were. . . ."[48] Winfield Townley Scott saw Horgan as stretching his 1948 *Cosmopolitan* story of the same title into a novel of lesser importance than his final prewar novel, *The Common Heart.*[49] Arthur Mizener termed the book an "unrealized novel," saying "the novel's sensibility operates at a level just above cliché."[50]

As for the reception of *Memories of the Future*, nine years later, most reviewers panned it. Peter Buitenhuis reduced the novel to a "curiosity" of confusing character names, a "coterie novel" of "cheerful ceremoniousness" with little evidence of "universal experience."[51] Tom Greene found the plot too contrived, saying, "One gets the unsettling feeling that we have here more of a plot outline for an interesting motion picture than a living, enduring novel."[52] *Catholic World* found Horgan too "misty-eyed" and "so in love with the whole naval mystique that one is reminded of those service films of the thirties with titles like . . . 'Annapolis Salute.' "[53] Others found it too genteel, dated, and melodramatic; but Venetia Pollock was most critical: "Much high flown sentiment about pride of arms and the glory of courage is bandied around but all I felt was disgust at the way they [the characters] wallowed in sorrow to hide their guilty relief at having survived."[54]

Although Buitenhuis, for one, overstates his case, he like Mizener points to a central issue in Horgan's military novels—how to reconcile the homefront and its civility with the horrors of the battlefield.

Horgan, because of the high proportion of social satire and "manners," does not succeed in relating tea cups and drawing rooms to bullets and death, but attempt it he does. There was a home front and a front line, after all, and Horgan dramatizes their interrelationships. If his World War II novels are not altogether convincing they have within them some of the potential that he more successfully achieves in *Trumpet* (1960), his most unique of all Westerns.

The Richard trilogy. Any excessive sentiment that marrs Horgan's novels about World War II is easily discounted as an aberration when considering his performance in the Richard trilogy. Horgan's purpose, as well as execution, in these novels, is a sterling one. Viewed as novels about the artist as a young man in New York and New Mexico in the 1920s. *The Fault of Angels* (1933) and *No Quarter Given* (1935) share a close thematic kinship with the Richard trilogy, three novels that again use autobiographical devices which parallel Horgan's growing up in the East and Southwest with the life of his fictive protagonist Richard. Thirty years after his first two novels, in the Richard trilogy—*Things As They Are* (1964), *Everything to Live For* (1968) and *The Thin Mountain Air* (1977)—Horgan again recounts the individual and family history of a young artist discovering his art and dedicating himself to the affirmation of humanity. If *No Quarter* at least partially incorporates *Angels*, then the Richard trilogy, more directly than Horgan's other novels, subsumes them both as his most significant effort as a transcontinental American novelist.

Each of the "Richard" novels is a self-contained work. Together they are a continuing story of the maturation of one person, Richard (his last name is unknown), from early childhood through adolescence into adulthood. Similarly, *Things As They Are* may be read as ten self-contained incidents or stories, since many of the chapters were first published as short stories; but they also form an organic whole. As such, it offers a kind of paradigm for the component construction of the trilogy. *Everything to Live For* has no chapter divisions as such—merely an extended story of a crisis summer in Richard's adolescence. *The Thin Mountain Air* is constructed in a box design of five chapters and an epilogue, a refinement of the interpolations of *No Quarter Given*, *The Common Heart*, and *Mexico Bay*. Throughout the trilogy the past of youth exists through memory and the retrospective narration of an older Richard writing at a distance of half a century, which places the Richard persona at the approximate age of Horgan as author. Again, the murallike design so characteristic of Horgan is within each novel and across all three.

Critics have not dealt in detail with these three novels as a group. Published over a period of thirteen years, the trilogy has elicited mostly individual attention with only passing comparisons. *Things As They Are* was hailed as a first-rate work; *Everything to Live For* did not fare well with some reviewers; *The Thin Mountain Air* received an average rating. The trilogy has been greeted with responses that range from adulation to glib dismissal.

Richard Boeth found the plot of *Mountain Air* a "cartoon-like procession" of episodes, and found Richard's rite of passage melodramatic and his innocence puzzling, "even disorienting, as we try to separate young Richard's perceptions from those of old Richard, the narrator, and either or both of these from Horgan's."[55] If one reviewer found Horgan's focus "indeterminate," another found the novel clichéd: "Like many novels about reaching manhood . . . the book has a hard core of triteness which even a fine technique cannot conceal."[56] Jack Sullivan thought it overloaded with epiphanies and revelations and the characters lifeless and unconvincing; but he believed "Horgan's sense of place . . . as palpable and magical as ever."[57] Ivan Gold took a more positive view and credited Horgan with "an elegant yet unobtrusive prose in which the events of the novel seem embedded, unfolding before the reader almost as if he were watching the action in a . . . Japanese scroll."[58]

Everything to Live For met a less fortunate fate than *Mountain Air* in the eyes of some reviewers. James F. Cotter pronounced it banal: "This novel falls on its face."[59] Guy Davenport called the story plausible Muzak, "fiction . . . written to serve the more sluggish of imaginations while satisfying various curiosities about the rich."[60] Representative of favorable response is Alfred C. Ames who considered the novel an "elegant work of art . . . both modern in its psychological penetration and its exemplification of the new social mores, and classical in its deliberate, chiseled phrasing and the simple directness of its plotting."[61]

Things As They Are charmed most reviewers. But it too evoked sarcasm in some readers. Margaret Parton termed the book poor Richard's "miserable little almanac," the product of "whine" and "self-pity."[62] More typical of the book's favorable reception are the words of Virgilia Peterson who judged it Horgan's best novel to that time: "Nothing he has written before quite foreshadows the piercing beauty of this latest novel."[63] *Newsweek* said, "It works."[64] And James Kraft, in a perceptive essay, placed the novel in the tradition of such classics of the maturation novel as the *Adventures of Huckleberry Finn, The Catcher in the Rye*, and *Portrait of The Artist.*[65]

Like any author, Horgan has his favorable and unfavorable readers. And for those who read *with* him rather than against him, the Richard trilogy works in marvelous ways and, taken as a whole, might be judged his finest achievement in the novel form. The trilogy is an ideal way of knowing Horgan's voice in fiction. A consideration of Richard's story and stance, his "autobiography" and how he tells it across the three novels, calls for both backward and forward glances from last novel to first, and from first novel to last. Such is the perspective, memory, and anticipation of Horgan through Richard.

As with all autobiographical narrative, fact and fiction, the end of Richard's life is not yet known. Richard does not die like Edmund Abbey in *No Quarter* (1935), although death, as a part of life, is very much on Richard's mind. He tells about his father's death in *Mountain Air*; about his cousin's death in *Everything to Live For*; his grandfather's and his uncle's deaths in *Things As They Are.* Other deaths are experienced too and have their impact on Richard—Buz Rennison, Don Elizario Wenzel, and Christopher St. Brides in *Mountain Air*; Richard's friend John Burley, and his kitten, in *Things As They Are*; the dalmation, Chief, in *Everything to Live For.* Even the "offstage" death of his family's German cook and Richard's childhood protectress, Anna, is subtly prominent as an indicator of time's passing in *Mountain Air.*

In addition to knowing about the deaths of his friends and family, Richard, one learns at the end of the trilogy, is a physician as his father always wished he would be when he nicknamed him "Doc" as a young boy. Just before his death, Richard's father asks him to promise to finish medical school and that promise is kept. He is a writer of books, too, as he says outright in the final novel. Although he never says which books he has authored, one knows that he has compiled from notes, taken habitually during the course of the action, the very autobiographical novels being read.

That Richard is destined to become an artist of some kind, be it painter, actor, or author, one knows from the start—given his ability to "see" life. Implicitly, one knows Richard is an artist by the very self-consciousness of his performance with words, his manner of expression. That he cares for humanity enough to follow some profession devoted to helping it—perhaps a priest (which he almost decides to become as a child), or a doctor—is likewise always known. The implied reader of the Richard trilogy is an intimate, a friend of Richard's, an extension of his very private yet public self who can appreciate the confessions Richard makes, the beautiful ways in which he orders what he is saying, the common humanity shared with a narrator/persona who senses the pain and the joy of being human.

Richard also is a soldier. Born just before World War I, Richard is too young to know that war firsthand, but he does recount poignantly, by means of the frame narration of *Mountain Air*, his time spent as an officer and courier in World War II. The time of *Things As They Are* begins about 1908 or 1909, with Richard's memories as a boy of four or five, and extends to World War I. In addition to being a physician, writer, and soldier, Richard is also a husband and father by the time he looks back at his life. Although the trilogy may end, Richard's life does not. And there are many parts of his life, namely, most of the years past his early twenties, for his reader to wonder about. Such is the expansive nature of the trilogy's autobiographical form.

Not only for the sake of drawing comparisons between author and personae, but for the sake of understanding Richard's character, it is important to point out that Richard is Catholic, with a strong sense of right and wrong, of sin and forgiveness, of the fallibility of man. His moral struggles play no small part in the action and ideas of the trilogy. He is also of combined German and Irish ancestry. Such a genealogy and heritage play a prominent part in understanding Richard's family, the history of which is chronicled throughout the trilogy, determining the way he meets life. A sense of family—its loves, values, and continuities—is an important theme in the Richard series, one that extends, as it does in much of Horgan's writing, to the family of man. Certainly Richard's philosophical and religious values, as well as certain aspects of his living East and West, seem to approximate many of Horgan's own. Others naturally do not. It is clear, however, that Horgan's voice as heard in the Richard series is characteristically that of artist and humanist.

It is important to think in terms of voices and personae in these novels insofar as they change—Richard changes and so does the society and the landscape—from book to book. The tone and style of each installment changes as Richard grows. *Things As They Are* (1964) is childlike, naively truthful although subtly knowledgeable at the same time. It is the perspective of a child, from the age of four to twelve, as he sees the world of Dorchester, but it is a perspective screened through that of an older man remembering how it was. Such a stance is difficult to convincingly attain in fiction—how to mix innocence with experience in just the right way. But Horgan is successful in uniting the two perspectives. *Everything to Live For* (1968) is stylistically more impetuous, "romantic," and sophisticated though broodingly and transparently so. It is the stance of adolescence, of Richard's seventeenth summer when he experiences on "vacation" the obsessive death wish and suicide of his cousin and his first sexual love, seen through a persona writing forty years later. The ambiance is that of the early 1920s, just after World War I, in the almost Gothic luxuriousness of eastern Pennsylvania. *Mountain Air* (1977) has a more complicated, bemused stylistic texture, as Richard tries to find himself, moving in the process from his home in Dorchester to Albuquerque and the even more remote San Augustín plains, southwest of Albuquerque, and a sheep ranch near Magdalena. Here the northeastern Anglo-American meets the Hispanic, the urban confronts the rural.

Richard becomes a man of high moral and aesthetic principles because of his family. Like Edmund Abbey, and John O'Shaughnessy in *Angels* (1933), he incorporates his life experiences into his art and makes, as his autobiographical narratives prove, art out of his life. The mutual love expressed between Richard, his father, Dan, and his mother, Rose (the names of Horgan's parents, too), and his other relatives is a strong stabilizing force throughout the trilogy. All three books are a tribute to his father and what he meant to Richard in his life and death.

The trilogy is an account of the peace Richard comes to make with himself and his own strengths and shortcomings through making a similar peace with his father's successes and failures, good deeds and bad. Richard's mother, too, is responsible for driving fear out of his life, through such "simple" things as facing a lightning storm; but she helps in more comprehensive ways through her love for her husband and son. As an observer of the worlds his parents establish for him—their homes in New York and New Mexico, the visits they arrange for him at his wealthy cousin's mansion in Pennsylvania and on the Wenzel ranch in New Mexico—he attempts to bring order and purpose to his life. As an autobiographer he is doing this again in a new way, bringing another kind of order, a recorded order, to his own life and to his parents' lives.

The concept is similar to what David L. Minter calls the principle of "interpreted design" in American literature, an idea Minter finds common to American autobiographers and novelists. Minter explains,

> The term *interpreted design* is intended . . . as a kind of metaphor for . . . works structured by juxtaposition of two characters, one a man of design or designed action . . . who dominates the action of his world, the other a man of interpretation . . . through whose interpreting mind and voice the story of the man of design comes to us.[66]

Minter's is a complex genre study with ramifications for all of American literature and for the literary types within which Horgan works, fiction and nonfiction, novel and biography. Suffice it to say that a reading of Richard as a portrait of the American artist as a young man is aided by considering him (and Horgan behind him) as a man of interpretation, always looking, always observing, always ordering individual, family, and larger social relationships—particularly those of artists and lovers—and trying to make something out of the actions of men and women of design.

A large part of what Richard must come to realize is how and why the things that he sees and knows, truths for him, are somehow not really "things as they are" for others. Much of the irony and impact of *Things As They Are* involves this conflict and the fact that Richard really does see right to the heart of things. No hypocrisy. No lies.

The trilogy opens when the world is all before him and his parents, long before his father's tuberculosis, with these words: " 'Richard, Richard,' they said to me in my childhood, 'when will you begin to see things as they are?' "[67] Each successive volume in the trilogy involves the compromise Richard has to make between his truths and those of others, and how there is a truth of sorts in lies. The trilogy ends with this question, spoken to Richard by his mother after his father's death: " 'Wouldn't it be wonderful not to have to make the best of things?' "[68] The world is no longer newly before him and his family. His father became lieutenant governor and almost governor of New York and could have carried it off magnificently had tuberculosis not exiled him to New Mexico where he, like Edmund

Abbey, partially recovers only to die just when his grand political design is within months of coming true. From not seeing things as they really are, to having to make the best of things, is what Richard tries to interpret in his life and reconstruct in his autobiography. Given the certainty of the mutual love of Richard and his parents, any disloyalty in that love, and by extension other loves, is disturbing to Richard. And it is just such betrayals of love and trust—whether in romantic love or friendship—which he must interpret and justify. When, in *Mountain Air*, his father reveals to him that he has loved not only Richard's mother but her best friend and Richard's childhood "love," a beautiful lady who smells of violets and whom he calls Aunt Bunch, Richard is not completely devastated. For that matter, neither is his mother when she finds out about her husband's secret love by yielding to the temptation of opening her husband's mail. It is not the first time Richard has seen "things as they are," seen betrayal in human love; but it is the time which confirms in a far from simple way that love is not intended to be selfish.

All of the other instances of betrayal in the trilogy culminate in his father's confession about having a mistress. As highly principled as his father is in business and politics, he is vulnerable like other men. Thus, when Richard retires to his willow grove by the Rio Grande and reads, as instructed, his father's letters to Aunt Bunch (before destroying them for his father), his own night of debauchery above the Marigold Café in Magdalena with the waitress, Larraine, and the drifter, Buz Rennison, is partially absolved in his father's guilt. Rennison's more serious crimes of murdering the old rancher and Richard's "patron," Don Elizario Wenzel, and raping Concha, Don Elizario's young wife—such uncontrolled acts of betrayal and violation witnessed in disbelief and a certain loss of faith by Richard, come to be reconciled as the other "shadow side" of human nature.

Moreover, Richard's voyeuristic interlude, on the eve of the family's forced departure for New Mexico, takes on related significance. Trying to know Dorchester before having to leave it, Richard goes in winter to the docks of the city harbor. He wants to escape from the new responsibilities he must face in helping his father back to health. There he sees a young man and woman living together on the summer steamer, the "Inland Queen." The couple's love offers the promise of freedom to him. He lusts to live with them—in blind anticipation of his actually joining the Steerforth-like Buz and the earthy Larraine. The dwellers on the "Inland Queen" die in a fire and through his vicarious reveries of escape with them, conceivably even in their deaths, he privately betrays his father and his mother in their need.

Arcing back from the sight of things as they are with his father's loyalty and betrayal in his love for both wife and mistress, is Richard's loss of virginity with Marietta Osborne after his cousin Max Chittenden's death in *Everything to Live For.* He loves Marietta almost from the beginning of that summer of death when he watches his Byronic cousin Max love and simultaneously hurt both his fiancée, Marietta, and his mother, Alicia. Richard watches Max try to destroy everything that love and privilege give him to live for; watches him perversely drive his speedy Isotta-Fraschini over the carcass of his own dog and into an oncoming freight train. As things would have it, Richard, in that summer of 1921, watches his older cousin turn from everything he himself wished he were into an urn of cremated ashes emptied into the darkly beautiful water of the quarry where Max always swam and which seemed his natural home. In a wounded state Richard prays, "Lord, keep me safe from powers I do not understand. Let me never destroy any loving thing in the name of lost love."[69]

The Richard trilogy, like its predecessors in his autobiographical fiction, reveals Horgan as very much the artist behind the artists he writes about, an artist who loves the stories that humanity in its individual and social ambitions creates in the living and in the telling.

Whitewater. Next to *A Distant Trumpet* (1960), *Whitewater* (1970) is Horgan's most widely recognized novel. Published three decades after *Main Line West* (1936), *A Lamp on the Plains* (1937), and *Far From Cibola* (1938), it is both a revisitation and an extension of his early plains novels. The young friends who make up the central trio of characters—Billy Breedlove, Marilee Underwood, and Phillipson Durham—and the moral choices which they face in growing up are reminiscent of the problems faced by Danny Milford and Kathleen McGraw and her brothers. The accidental deaths of Billy Breedlove, Stephen McGraw, and Franz Vosz add to the similarity of key events in Horgan's prewar and postwar plains novels.[70] More explicitly, *Whitewater* makes use of and is influenced by Horgan's folk opera, *A Tree On the Plains* (1943).

When the novel opens, Phillipson Durham no longer lives in the town of Belvedere near Whitewater Lake on the plains of west-central Texas. He is a humanist, a professor of literature, a specialist on William Beckford, involved with the talk and writing of his students. He does not work for Belvedere Printers as did his father. He is married and a father. But the people and place of Belvedere, the pain and joy of his youth there, are still very much with him in memory. And the novel, framed by glimpses of Durham during the day as a teacher in discussion with his students and at night as a musing family man, is a resurrection of his youth on the plains. Seen as sequel to *Lamp*, it is as if Danny Milford has grown up to become professor Durham.

Although autobiographical in its narration, the novel is not so much told by Durham, as it is revealed, lyrically, through his thoughts as his older self looks back at his younger self. Point of view is important because it is reinforced imagistically and symbolically by means of several types of landmarks throughout the novel. The network of relationships, direct and associative, between Horgan's retrospective narrative techniques and place in time and space is subtle and extensive. The flatness, the dryness, dust, and heat, and the vistas of distance which give a sweeping horizontal axis to the novel are crossed by the verticality of the town water tower and Whitewater lake. Durham is attempting to see his vanished past, the events and people, his guilt and his gratitude, by looking back over time and down into his very soul. The effect is elegiac.

The town of Belvedere is as much buried by the years of Durham's past as the town of Whitewater is covered by Whitewater Lake. And the voices of his dead friends, Billy and Marilee, of his parents, of the banker Tom Bob Gately, of the state patrolman Hardy Jo Stiles, of his benefactress, Victoria Cochran—all of these voices are long faded like the anonymous voices he and Billy once heard on Fifth Island on Whitewater Lake. But the voices of those plains people are heard again in the voices of his students, the voices of his present life. For the interlude which is the novel, a night, a lifetime, Durham relives his youth.

What has marked Durham most and what serves as dual climactic episodes in the novel are the deaths, related in love, of his high school friends. Only by following the counsel of the wealthy, free-thinking widow, Victoria Cochran, does Durham spiritually survive his part in the accidental death of Billy and the subsequent suicide of Marilee. " 'Promise me never to try *not* to think about what happened,' " Victoria advises.[71] She tells him this, significantly, not inside her book and painting-filled mansion at Crystal Wells Farm, but in her car. Together they ride over the plains, purging their sorrow in their own way and deliberately avoiding Billy's funeral of "organized mortuary horrors" (*W*, 252).

That ride with Victoria is a restorative one, a tribute to Billy, to the plains, and to all plains people. It is Victoria who introduces Durham to *Vathek* and the life of William Beckford and "ordains" him a humanist. In their seemingly casual discussions about Beckford's towering residence at Fonthill Abbey is the implication of Phillipson's future and more subliminally of Billy's fall in his aspiring climb to paint "Beat Orpha City" on the Belvedere water tower—and even of Marilee's suicide by drowning in Whitewater Lake, pregnant and forsaken in her love.

Reviews of *Whitewater* are among the most provocative of any written about Horgan's writing. James Boatwright found Victoria Cochran's advice to Phillipson that he "transform the commonplace into the legendary" and try "to find the beauty behind the banality" the generating forces of the novel.[72] Charles Newman thought the novel both fascinating and boring, an example of "how fluid the novel form has become," writing which is "neither traditional nor post-modern."[73] Denis Donoghue thought Billy Breedlove too much a barbarian to love and Victoria Cochran too full of moral platitudes and impeccable taste—and Horgan too abstractly concerned about Man over people.[74]

In all their comments—pro and con—reviewers proved *Whitewater* characteristic of Horgan's provocative powers as a novelist. The realism inherent in his novels, early and late, in his powers to relate what he "sees" in lives and landscapes, is part and parcel of his faith in both God and man. Those who do not side with proponents of "moral fiction," who like Jamake Highwater believe that straightforward story telling is obsolete in postmodern times because "faith in the West is obsolete,"[75] will likely dismiss Horgan categorically. But those like John Gardner who believe that the function of fiction is to preserve faith should see Horgan as an author who has pulled his own weight and the tradition of realistic fiction as far as any twentieth-century American novelist. In *Mexico Bay* Horgan yet once again confirms that tradition.

Mexico Bay. Reviewers generally agreed that *Mexico Bay* (1982) represents a worthy capstone to Horgan's fiction.[76] Jonathan Yardley observed, "It has an air that is at once nostalgic and elegaic, as though Horgan were harking back to a lost time that has particular and profound meaning for him. In the best sense of the term it is an 'old man's book,' one that looks to the past with affection, pride and clarity."[77] Johanna Kaplan stressed the importance of the heroine, Diana Macdonald Wentworth, as the focal point of the narrative, and concluded, ". . . above all, though somewhat swaddled by less than vivid language and by distinctly mannered locutions, what this novel offers is a wonderful story."[78] Richard James, taking an opposite tack, said, "If the characters . . . do not seem heroic, and if the story leans too heavily on chance, the reader is nonetheless rewarded by the nocturnes of Horgan's fluid, nearly impeccable prose."[79] All in all, the book was greeted with fondness for an old friend.

His latest novel to date, *Mexico Bay* proves Horgan a bold and beautiful exception to W. Somerset Maugham's generalization that authors reach the height of their powers between the ages of thirty-five and forty.[80] Although he has had obvious early, middle, and late phases in his life and his writing, Horgan, nearing eighty on the publication of this novel, has lost none of the magic, none of his sensitivity to structure and sentence, pattern and rhythm, that was present when he won the Harper prize novel contest for his first novel, *The Fault of Angels*, in 1933; when he achieved one of his most impressive and organic unions of form and content with *Far From Cibola* in 1938; when he sustained so beautifully the lyricism of *Whitewater* in 1970; or when, with *The Thin Mountain Air* in 1977, he finished his poignant account of growing up, the Richard trilogy.

One of the truly significant things about *Mexico Bay* as the latest installment in Horgan's long list of novels is that it highlights not just his own ability as a novelist in the realistic tradition, it brings to mind, as well, in the very fabric of the novel itself—its action and theme—his career as a Pulitzer-prize winning historian and biographer, and as an amateur painter. In addition to being consistent and prolific, Horgan, over the years, has been versatile. And his claim to being a true humanist and American man of letters—all the truer for the scarcity of the breed—may be seen to culminate in *Mexico Bay* wherein Horgan's own experiences with the theater, with literature, with painting, and with the military life all converge masterfully. Always one to incorporate in varying degrees his own biography into his art, *Mexico Bay*—in some ways and particularly at this late-life stage the most comprehensively biographical of all his works—offers support for the assertion that Horgan, as man and author infused into the composites which here make up his four main characters, is his own best hero. To say this is not so much a matter of ego as it is art.

To emphasize a major contention of this study, as a novelist and as a historian Horgan is simultaneously regional and transcontinental. The great American themes of the East's contact with the West both in terms of the settling of the frontier and of the West's backtrailing to the East have always preoccupied him. And so it is again in *Mexico Bay* which takes as its locale such diverse and shifting settings as Texas, Iowa, up-state New York, Washington, D.C., Georgetown, and Canada—all well-known places to Horgan in his lifetime. But it is the Gulf of Mexico, especially the areas around Brownsville and Boca Chica at the mouth of the Rio Grande, and the city and bay of Corpus Christi, which provide the nodality of place and motive for the story. For it is there, at "Mexico Bay," and not war-time Washington as some reviewers insist, that the lives of the book's characters dramatically cross and recross, in terms of the story's present and in terms of the historical past of the Mexican War of 1846–1848, and the sixteenth-century explorations of Sir Francis Drake and the mappings of his navigator, invented by Horgan and named for the purposes of the novel, Nicholas Broughton.

Some, as mentioned, read *Mexico Bay* as the fictionalized biography of young, beautiful, and wealthy Dorchester, New York socialite Diana MacDonald Wentworth and of her adventures and misadventures with four men: her father, George MacDonald, a wealthy newspaper publisher who fought with Pershing in his punitive expedition against Pancho Villa in 1916 and who dies on a courier mission off the coast of South America in World War II; John Wentworth, the older-man and debonair playwright whom she marries as a surrogate father and then leaves for much the same reason; Benjamin Ives, an Iowa farm boy become free-spirited painter who after adopted patronage by Wentworth and coercion into a curiously malicious and tempting *ménagé-a-trois* whisks Diana off to the wildly irresponsible and happy beaches of the Gulf where although he leads her to independence he leaves her with sorrowful memories of his profligacy and his violent death; and, last, her eventual deliverer and solace, Howard Debler, an academic whose two passions, to write a definitive history of the Mexican War and to marry Diana, are realized only after years of waiting out the war, and after a climactic series of harrowing escapes and chases. Read this way, *Mexico Bay* does have a kind of budding feminist relevancy to the story's present of the pre and postwar 1930s and 1940s.

Surely Diana Wentworth is convincing as woman and as type. But it is really the men in the book, Horgan's heroes as it were, who prove most fascinating—on their own terms, again as men and as types, but most especially in their relationships with each other as they vie in turn for Diana's affections. Horgan has dealt fleetingly and sensitively with homosexuality before, most notably in *Whitewater* (1970), and he has seemingly always been interested in male friendship and companionship, so that a litany of his fiction's male companions (whether soldiers, artists, or children), usually foils of weak and strong, intellectual and physical, subservient and dominant, could easily be recited. And Horgan has often utilized the lovers' triangle to great effect in his novels. One need only think of *The Fault of Angels, No Quarter Given, The Common Heart, Whitewater*, and *The Thin Mountain Air* in this regard. But never has he been quite so provocative, so ambiguous yet explicit, about the physical/spiritual attractions that can exist between two men as he is here in the network of rivalry, jealousy, and voyeurism which he constructs (by means of violence and nakedness) between John Wentworth and Benjamin Ives. In many ways this is one of the most erotic and sexual of Horgan's novels and invites the somewhat errant thought that perhaps like E. M. Forster's posthumous fiction there are homosexual motifs in Horgan's works that one day will be discovered and discussed more fully.

Ultimately, however, in terms of character, this is Howard Debler's book. He seems Horgan's closest counterpart. Horgan's consciousness. His own best hero. It doesn't take much distortion of the boundaries of fiction and biography to see Debler as Horgan, working away, in method and in perception on the *magnum opus, Great River*: the years of research, the interruption of the war, the field notes, the flourishes of word-pictures when it comes to evoking the sublime moods and the magnitude of the great Southwestern landscape, riverscape, and gulfscape. Debler is victorious, nobly and happily so, in his quest for success in his writing and in his life. He has his mother on his side (a minor but endearing character in her obsession with neatness), and he has in his home and heritage in Grand Plains, Texas (near Amarillo) from which he sallies forth like others of Horgan's plains people to do battle with the small and large evils and failures of life—in drawing rooms, in nature, in world war—and to which he retreats alone to write and then with Diana for healing and restoration. As a tall Texan in love with the West as place and as idea, as story and history, he has his antecedents in much of Horgan's fiction, most particularly Dr. Rush in *The Common Heart.*

For Debler and for Horgan the notion of the Gulf of Mexico, or as Drake's navigator calls it in the epigraph from which the novel takes its title, "Mexico Bay," amounts to inspiration, amounts to a metaphor for the awesome riddles involved in any artist's journey toward art. Readers can be thankful that Horgan as novelist is still in passage, W. Somerset Maugham notwithstanding.

Chapter Three

Shorter Fiction

Augmenting Horgan's major achievement as a novelist is his equally prolific ability as an author of novellas and short stories. His combined talents in both the novel and shorter fiction complement each other to the degree that it is ill advised to speculate on which form most influences the other. Rather it is best to regard him as a fictionist at home with both long and short narratives. During his beginnings as a novelist in the 1930s he also wrote many works of shorter fiction. His collected shorter fiction runs close to forty titles and a tally of uncollected titles would run the total past the hundred mark. Much of his uncollected shorter fiction is hidden away in forgotten issues of magazines like *Mademoiselle* (1935); *Ladies' Home Journal* (1936); the *Saturday Evening Post* (from the late 1940s through the mid 1960s Horgan published twenty or so stories and excerpts in the *Post*); *Cosmopolitan* (1947–51); *Good Housekeeping* (1947–51); *McCall's* (1949); *Collier's* (1950–53); and in more "intellectual" publications like the *Yale Review* (his first published short story, "The Head of the House of Wattleman," later incorporated in *The Fault of Angels*, appeared in the *Yale Review* in 1929—a journal which accepted many of his stories and reviews for more than a decade, including "The Peach Stone" [1942] and "Taos Valley" [1944]); *Harpers Magazine* (1931–42); the *North American Review* (1932–36); the *New Yorker* (1933–34); *Scribner's* (1935); the *Atlantic Monthly* (1938); *Saturday Review* (1942); and in obscure and long-defunct publishing ventures like B. A. Botkin's University of Oklahoma attempt at promoting regional writing, *Folk-Say* (1929–32).

Many of Horgan's collected stories come originally from these magazines and journals. And excerpts from his novels also appeared in them. Furthermore, he contributed poetry and essays to them and to other periodicals—including *Poetry: A Magazine of Verse* ("Exotics" [1924], "The Mask" [1925], "Westward" [1933]); the *South-*

west Review (1933–55); and the *New Mexico Quarterly* (1936–54).[1]

Uncollected or collected, in print and out, excerpted or used in novels, none of Horgan's short fiction is artless.[2] Even his stories written for popular audiences of "slick" magazines such as the *Post* and others through the 1930s and into the 1960s reveal careful technique and craftsmanship. In seeking to supplement his salary at the New Mexico Military Institute before World War II and in making his living as a writer after the war, Horgan never compromised his artistic talent in writing for popular markets which his agent, Virginia Rice, helped him find. With so much short fiction to his name there is an inevitable degree of unevenness, but not enough to keep readers of both middle-brow and high-brow tastes from wishing that all of his shorter fiction was more accessible.

An examination of the uncollected stories shows that many of them qualify as high caliber instances of short story–novella forms. Among the best are "The Witch" and "The Burden of Summer" (*Folk-Say* [1930, 1932]); two stories in *Harpers,* "In A Winter Dusk" (1931), and "Comedy on the Plains" (1941); three in the *North American Review*: "Point of Honor" (1932), "Surgical Crisis" (1933), and "A Journey of Hope" (1936). Others, though somewhat clichéd, offer much more than mere pot-boiler entertainment. A sampling of these would include: "A Fragment of Empire" (*Ladies Home Journal* [1936]), and four *Post* stories: "I Came to Kill" (1954), "Unexpected Hero" (1953), "Wall of Flame" (1959), and "Rain in Laredo" (1963). The subjects and themes of his uncollected stories, like his collected short fiction (and his novels), deal with brujas, writers, painters, frontiersmen, soldiers, hashslingers, professors—diverse individuals and families in all sorts of predicaments, tragic and comic, in the distant and recent historical past. Pervasive is his familiar humanistic affirmation. William T. Pilkington finds it ironic that some of Horgan's best works are also some of his shortest.[3] More surprising than ironic is the way that Horgan's shortest fiction complements not only his novels but his nonfiction, making his work an integrated whole.

Luckily, some of his shorter fiction is relatively easy to find. And it is with the four volumes of his collected shorter fiction that any critical consideration must begin: *The Return of the Weed* (1936), *Figures in a Landscape* (1940), *Humble Powers* (1955), and *The*

Peach Stone (1967). Other short fiction, including *The Saintmaker's Christmas Eve* (1955), is of related interest. Together these volumes represent about thirty short stories, five novellas, or—as the subtitle to *The Peach Stone* indicates—the "stories from four decades." Before anything is said about the lives and the landscapes represented in these stories, it is important to remark generally on each of his four major collections of short fiction.

The Return of the Weed is the result of the collaborative efforts of friendship: six stories by Horgan and six lithographs by Peter Hurd.[4] As the title suggests, the unifying theme of the book is mutability, the constant physical and spiritual battle of man against time's relentless ruinations. In his recognition of the struggle, Horgan's hope for humanity is nevertheless sanguine as seen in his comments which frame the stories by way of "Argument" and "Resolution."

Horgan's idea for these stories came from one line in a 1916 U.S. government report on New Mexico which in part stated that on the land there were "Visible Evidences of Failure." Each story stresses this defeat of men and women by the land and focuses on some visible ruin, some monument to a past effort and reputation. It is a "suite" design found in many of his works and not unlike Peter Hurd's *South Plains Mural* in its rendering of the lives and landscapes on the plains which Horgan and Hurd knew together.[5]

When *The Weed* was published in 1936 Horgan was thirty-three years old, acclaimed for *The Fault of Angels* (1933), established as a more than one book author with *No Quarter Given* (1935), and waiting with his third novel, *Main Line West* (1936). One reviewer felt Horgan's narratives slight, more interested in theme than in action or character.[6] Reviews considered Horgan too lyrical, too much the poet, and predicted little success for the book. In 1980 *The Weed* was hailed as a Southwestern "classic."[7]

Another "suite" or "mural," *Figures in a Landscape* (1940) is a fusion of story and essay, a book that takes the "Argument"/"Resolution" method of *The Weed*, and expands it by alternating essay with story.[8] Like *The Weed* it is an early example of Horgan's inclination to reshape generic boundaries of fiction and nonfiction.

Such an enterprise naturally raises questions of unity, and readers have varying views on his success in achieving it. Certainly the stories can stand alone without his asides. Some of the stories originally did stand alone, and five out of nine stories appear in yet another thematic context in *The Peach Stone*. But most readers will find his "essays" in *Landscape* indispensable. Much of what he says in these interpolated essays he said completely and uninterrupted in his seminal essay, "About the Southwest." This essay and thus *Landscape* anticipate Horgan's panoramic masterwork, *Great River.* As early as 1929 and 1931 Horgan published two prose-murals in *Folk-Say*: "Episodes from the Passionate Land" and "Figures in a Landscape." Both provided early bases for later "panoramic" prose works—including *Figures in a Landscape, From the Royal City*, and *The Centuries of Santa Fe.* Horgan's liking for trilogies and triptychs might be traced to these early "prose murals."

Like *The Weed*, the landscape is that of the Southwest, western Texas and southeastern New Mexico; and the lives are those of Native American, Hispanic, and Anglo-American introduced over three centuries and specifically seen in the nineteenth and twentieth centuries. The concern is with man's enduring spirit across space and time.

Reviewers of *Landscape* again concentrated on Horgan's style and design. The *New York Times* saw the pattern as the reason of being for the book but singled out some of the stories as inappropriate to the general design. This, coupled with what was judged an overliterary and mannered style "which contrasts unpleasantly with the directness of the actual tales," added up to the assessment of the book as an "interesting experiment," a book "planned with genuine inspiration," but a "noble failure."[9] Harry T. Moore judged *Landscape* "a fine and full picture of that fascinating melange of cultures which makes up New Mexico"; but also found the essay portions "too formally written to fit smoothly between the stories."[10] The murallike quality of the book did not escape the attention of *Time*'s reviewer as seen in references to "short panels of monologue giving the historical setting, sketching the traces of old times from which the author takes his scenes."[11]

Horgan's next collection of shorter fiction, *Humble Powers* (1955), brings together three novellas which initially appeared in the *Post* and *Cosmopolitan. The Devil in the Desert* (1950) is set in the Southwest. A second story, *One Red Rose for Christmas* (1951), takes place in the East; the third, *To the Castle* (1951), has wartime Italy as its setting. The notion of man's humble powers of, respectively, faith, love, and sacrifice, unifies these stories. Separately, however, the interrelationship between lives and landscapes works as a salient theme in itself. In his preface, Horgan says that the form of *Humble Powers* is a triptych "in the context of an uninterrupted and universal Christianity . . ." (*HP*, 7). In their Christian assumptions and messages, these religious stories are also complemented by another of his novellas of the same year, *The Saint Maker's Christmas Eve* (1955); and although not included in *Humble Powers*, it can be viewed as adding another panel to this particular instance of mural-like design.

Reviewers were undecided about what to call these stories. *Commonweal* refused to call *The Devil in the Desert* a novella, saying rather that it was a long short story—or as the publisher labeled it, a "legend," but a "pleasant and unusual story" in any event.[12] The *Saturday Review* referred to *One Red Rose* as a little fable in the tradition of Dickens's *A Christmas Carol*.[13] *The Saint Makers' Christmas Eve* was regarded a historical fable.[14] For Horgan they were a matter of religion and art, part of the same circle "when it enclosed that motive which sees devotion in all acts that attempt to capture the likeness of life" (*HP*, 8).

The Peach Stone (1967) contains twenty stories written from 1930 to 1966. Five stories were also previously included in *Landscape* and one novella, *The Devil in the Desert*, appeared as well in *Humble Powers*. *The Peach Stone* is a classic collection of Horgan's shorter fiction. As is the case with his other volumes of short fiction, a larger design is involved than just one story following another—although the chronological order in which the stories appeared is listed at the back of the volume. About the plan of the book he writes: "These stories from the varied backgrounds and experiences of my life—East and West, the historical past and the legendary present—are . . . grouped here in four parts. Part One brings together stories that speak primarily of childhood, Part Two of youth, Part Three of maturity, and Part Four of age."[15]

As with the titles of Horgan's other volumes of shorter fiction, *The Peach Stone* is emblematic of humanity's natural will to live. The four thematic parts of the volume reinforce the seasonal cycles of both lives and landscapes, Eastern and Western. Such a panorama reflects Horgan's own biography. One reviewer referred to the form of the book as Horgan's assembling of stories "in a colorful collage of his life" in "delicate cameo[s] carved from memory."[16] Another reviewer calls the form "creative in spirit, . . . far more than a repackaging of previously published work."[17]

These four volumes of collected shorter fiction, *The Return of the Weed, Figures in a Landscape, Humble Powers*, and *The Peach Stone* are only representative of Horgan's many short stories and novellas. One finds in his shorter fiction about the Southwest, Far West, and Northeast the artistic application and devotion of his humanist aesthetic that is devoted to exploring the light and darkness of the biographical and geographical regions of humankind. We may now consider more closely some of Horgan's shorter fiction.

Stories Southwest

Of the transcontinental regions Horgan writes about, the Southwest is the place which dominates his shorter fiction. More specifically, it is the historical past and the legendary present, as he calls them, of New Mexico which he maps. To read his Southwest stories is to read about eastern and northern New Mexico—the Pecos, Hondo, and Rio Grande valleys.

As in Hurd's *South Plains Mural*, Horgan's Southwestern prose-murals feature types of lives indigenous to the histories and cultures of the region from early Indian and Spanish colonial times through trader, cavalry, and cowboy times up to the mid-twentieth century. Just as the different landforms and climatic zones of the Southwest encompass deserts, rivers, plains, and mountains, so do the various lives and occupations common to the Southwest fill Horgan's stories: priests, nuns, doctors, lawyers, settlers, soldiers, ranchers, and merchants. Character—the history and biography of both person and place—becomes all important. To understand more fully Horgan's attitude, his own intuitive perceptions, of the interrelationships between lives and landscapes—history, biography, and geography—a brief look at his *Southwest Review* essay, "About the Southwest," provides an important starting point.

Historical panorama. Horgan begins "About the Southwest" with a view of the land shown in a 1679 French map that depicts the area now known as New Mexico, Texas, Arizona, and Oklahoma (in part). The Rio Grande is incorrectly shown as running north to the Pacific, and the Rocky Mountains are likewise inaccurate. In spite of these mistakes, Horgan calls the cartographer heroic. That he considers the Southwest identifiable with this questing resolve of the human spirit, be it that of the Conquistadors or Anglo-American settlers, is everywhere apparent in his stories and histories. In *Mexico Bay* (1982) the descriptions of the Gulf of Mexico as it was first charted by the pseudo-historical Nicolas Broughton, an imagined cartographer of Francis Drake, is Horgan's most recent up-dating of these early versions of map-maker as hero.

In speculating about the topography of mountains and plains in relationship to human settlement, Horgan insists that only human ingenuity and faith allowed homes to be made. The mercurial nature of the Rio Grande, from peaceful stream to flooding torrent, is emblematic of the Southwest for Horgan. Other determining characteristics of the region he lists as arroyo floods, the distance, the sun, and the challenge of the heat. All of these characteristics are transposed in image and metaphor to his fiction.

To the Pueblo Indians the upper Rio Grande was home. They were familiar with the flora and fauna. But to the European eye danger was everywhere, and the extremes of climate produced the need of a new philosophy. The strangeness of the country led first to fancy and then to legend. The European travelers came, made their reports, created a legend, and set in motion the irresistable social force of conquest and settlement. It is against this theme of settlement in a strange new world that Horgan examines what he calls the "heroic triad," the "laminated" cultures of Indian, Hispanic, and Anglo-American.

In such a historic context he places the Southwestern fiction of *Landscape* and other volumes. No single theme is more encompassing in his fiction than the theme of cultural settlement in the general terms of Frederick Jackson Turner's 1893 thesis of successive frontiers. In his essay, "The Significance of the Frontier in American History," Turner argued that "The existence of an area of free land, its continuous recession, and the advance of American settlement westward, explain American development."[18] Horgan seemingly subscribes to Turner's thesis.

Turner's successive frontiers may be seen as implicit panels in Horgan's continuing prose-mural from "About the Southwest," to *Landscape* and *New Mexico's Own Chronicle* (1937) which both incorporate that same essay, to *Great River* (1954) and *Lamy* (1975), his Pulitzer-Prize-winning histories. For both Turner and Horgan, Anglo-American assumptions about progress and civilization place prior cultures such as that of the Indian in the position of vestiges which must adapt to Anglo-American settlement or vanish. One can conjecture for this reason that Native American and Hispanic readers of the 1980s might judge Horgan as somewhat patronizing in his portrayals of Indians and Mexican Americans. This would not be fair to him, however, insofar as he was attempting as early as 1933, within the Anglo attitudes of that day, to break down stereotypes.

Early Historical past. Most of Horgan's stories set in the early historical past of the Southwest deal with the life of a priest and his struggles in bringing the Catholic faith to Indians. Horgan's attitude toward these early priests' missionary efforts, which involved not only bringing a new faith to the Indians but keeping their own faith intact, is sympathetic to the point of viewing the priests as heroic. Such a view of the priest figure as heroic traveler in an alien world culminates in his biography of Archbishop Jean Baptiste Lamy.

Horgan's priests as Christian humanists and men of peace cannot be considered apart from the Conquistadors, and the Indian lives they came to subjugate. None of his shorter fiction deals with the Indian before the coming of the Spanish conquerors. In histories like *Chronicle* and *Great River* the landscape before the Spanish invasion is portrayed through legends and myths, but in his short fiction the Indian is seen as vanquished by either Spanish or Anglo-American colonists. Horgan is not without sympathy for the dispossessed Indians. But as a Catholic who believes in the values of European humanism, and as an Anglo-American with faith in the progress of Western civilization, it is the priest and the Conquistador with whom Horgan identifies. This is apparent in several of his stories about priests in the early historical past.

"The Mission," the one story about the early historical past in *The Return of the Weed*, concerns the martyrdom of a Franciscan priest, Father Puig y Castaña, in the Pueblo rebellion of 1680. The story focuses on an autumn day in 1680 when, at the age of seventy and after thirty years of devoting his life to bringing his religion to the Indians in New Spain, he is murdered and the church he has worked so hard to build is burned in rebellion. Horgan suggests that there is a cycle in such a disaster, a vengeful one, in that the priest had first come during the destruction and killing of Indians by the Spanish who had, in 1650, burned the pueblo. For thirty years the priest had worked to rebuild the pueblo and to build his church out of dirt and clay: "The church rose with the city, and to the priest, the matter of using the mud of the earth to house humanity was a moving gesture" (*RW*, 7). Through memories the priest relives his life and work.

Horgan's portrayal of the priest's agonizing death at the hands of "murdering Indians" dramatizes not so much the priest's folly but his heroic endurance. Very much the human he says, "Do not kill me in the fields standing in the sunlight, in this beautiful autumn" (*RW*, 12). The fact that parts of the church cannot be destroyed, "the buttresses would stay mounded," is suggestive proof, even if in ruin, of the abiding continuation of his faith and work. Somehow his final request for God's forgiveness is granted. The church and what it represented of a life would be forever part of the landscape.

The murder of another priest and the lingering presence of his spirit is the theme of "The Isleta Priest," one of three vignettes found in "Episodes from the Passionate Land" published in *Folk-Say.* In addition, "The Fortress, 1772," one of several vignettes of "Taos Valley" published in the *Yale Review*, concerns the designing and building of the Mission of Saint Francis of Assisi by another Franciscan priest and humanist hero. The Isleta priest's coffin raises through the floor of the church—caused by the meandering currents of the nearby Rio Grande or by some miracle—as a terrifying reminder of the Indians' "sinful" acts. And the Taos valley priest's church is a monument to God's spirit in man blending with spirit of place: "In final humility, [the priest] never knew that the beauty of his purposes and reasons went into the walls three paces thick, the roof like a canyon rim, the buttresses like foothills, the light and shadow of a mesa; and was there to be seen ever after."[19]

A church, however, is not Christianity. And Horgan's humanism looks beyond the physical to the spiritual, beyond the building of churches to the vagabond ministries of priest as traveller. Two of his better known stories apply here: *The Devil in the Desert* (1952) and *The Saint Maker's Christmas Eve* (1955). The early historical pasts of these stories is the early and mid-nineteenth century, two centuries beyond the times of "The Mission" and a century beyond the church building of "The Fortress." In both stories an element of the miraculous enters into the resolution of the plot.

The Saint Maker's Christmas Eve involves brotherly love, trial in a snowstorm, divine guidance, and the blessing of a priest. The characters in this novella are seen by some as flat, "never ris[ing] above a fairy-tale level of existence; they never come alive. . . ."[20] And the story itself has been relegated to one of many "glib specimens of that genre of 'Christmas stories' seen each year. . . ."[21] This novella possesses more significance than such criticism suggests. It is a story about the making of an artist and the artist's intuition and imitation of

God's own acts of creation. Its message, in the Christmas tradition, is that God's love may be seen in man's art and in love of humanity. Such love, in act and artifact, is at once the most humble and the most saintly of all gifts.

The miraculous salvation takes place on Christmas Eve in 1809 near the northern New Mexico village of San Cristóbal. Saint Christopher appears in a snowstorm to guide a lost santero to safety. And the saintmaker's lost statute of Saint Christopher guides a lost priest out of the same storm. Both the saintmaker and the priest are reunited as old friends in San Cristóbal and the festivities surrounding the dedication of the statue continue through the telling of the miracles. To appreciate the true miracle of what transpired that night, the story must be viewed as starting fifteen years before, when three lives intersected at a propitious time and place. In keeping with the allegorical nature of the tale, Horgan suggests that the basis for the events began two thousand years before with the travels and gifts of the first Christmas. Just as that first Christmas affected countless others, so does that northern New Mexico Christmas affect a whole community of believers beyond the three persons whose lives are dramatized.

The three lives most directly influenced by the miracles of Christmas are Roberto Castillo, the santero or carver of wooden statues of saints called santos; Roberto's younger brother and partner, Carlos Castillo; and a traveling Franciscan father known first to them as a teacher of the craft of saintmaking and later known to Roberto on that San Cristóbal Christmas Eve as the father resident from the village of Santa Cruz. Horgan, through an omniscient narrator and then through the personae of Roberto and the priest, tells the miraculous story for the benefit of a skeptical and angry Carlos who at first wants only the payment for the St. Christopher statue but is softened by the humanizing explanation and news that from one donated santo have come orders for a half-dozen others.

The saintmaker of the title is Roberto for it is mainly his story—in the happening and in the telling. But Horgan is ambiguous in also making the Franciscan priest and the younger brother saintmakers, and not only in the literal sense of woodcarvers. The morality of the matter is reciprocal because if the santos take on their form and life in artistic imitation of the human form, humans take on their saintly stature in imitation of God, the santos, and the saintly lives they represent. The process of saintmaking, then, its craftsmanship and artistry, finds its reflection as much in living as in carving. Little does the Franciscan priest know at the time of his teaching that his lessons in the craft of saintmaking will transcend wood to reshape his very character and his relationship with God and man. Thus there are several kinds of saints and saintmakers in the story.

Like Father Louis Bellefontaine in *The Devil in the Desert*, the priest here is an irritable man when he first comes to the Castillo brothers' village. His irritability comes from his weakness and frustration in having so much to do and so few resources to do it with—among such poor people in such a remote land. He suffers his exile in such a hot and arid land with a matching dryness of soul when he comes for a fortnight to minister to the villagers of northern New Mexico. And this same anxious waiting for relief from his physical and spiritual exile continues fifteen years to his reunion with Roberto in San Cristóbal. What he has taught Roberto, however, as manifested in the statue of St. Christopher Roberto has carved and which guides him to safety, results in the regeneration of his spirit. In his own talents as a saintmaker, preacher, and teacher is his salvation.

Like the priest in "The Fortress," this priest is an artist and a builder, and his artistry is based humanistically on a love for people: "He was at his best with children and old people, for in the one he saw beginnings, and in the other, endings, both of which were closer to God, the source of the goal, and less trying than middles, when people thought they knew what they wanted."[22] To the priest, as to Horgan, a work of faith is the same thing as a work of art; and if in a dry piece of cottonwood is the waiting form of a saint, then in a man is the potential for saintliness.

As mentioned, Father Louis Bellefontaine is the name of the priest in *The Devil in the Desert.*[23] One critic sees this story as "strongly reminiscent of parts of Willa Cather's *Death Comes for the Archbishop*," with a central character much more "alive" than any in *The Saintmaker's Christmas Eve.*[24] It is widely considered to be Horgan's most successful priest story and among his best works of shorter fiction. Father Louis's life has been a long one of service to God and the people of the Rio Grande valley. He, like Horgan's other priests, is an exile—having come to the Southwest from France a generation before his fellow countryman and pastor, Father Pierre Arnoud. Although older, Father Louis is Father Pierre's assistant. They exist in a respectful, friendly though temperamental relationship somewhat similar in outline to the historical brotherhood of Jean Baptiste Lamy and Joseph Machebeuf.

The story begins in the historical past of "almost a hundred years ago," or around 1850 if one takes the narrator's present as 1950, the publication date of the story. The date is vague enough, however, to lend the story an air of legend. Father Louis, at the age of seventy and with thirty years of riding north, prepares for yet another trip up the river from the rectory located at Brownsville. The plot follows Father Louis's final ride. After reaching one of his northern-most stops, the home of Encarnadino Guerra, the priest continues his journey but, resting in the desert, is bitten by a snake and dies alone except for his horse. The horse eventually finds his way through the brush country back to Guerra's home. Despite Guerra's search, Father Louis's body is not found until eight years later, when Guerra comes across it by accident and returns to Father Pierre what possessions and relics remain from the ravages of the desert. Somewhat similar to the Castillo brothers, Guerra plays his supportive secular role with the humility and goodness that complements the saintlike qualities of both Father Louis, who is in effect martyred, and Father Pierre, who at the end of the story is a bishop elect returning to France—ending his exile in the Southwest.

Father Louis's journey north and his death are central to the story. But the interrelationships between the two priests and Guerra serve to highlight the significance of Father Louis's life and the way he meets death in the form of a diamond-back rattlesnake. Only the reader, through the omniscience of the narrator, is privy to the details of the fabulistic confrontation in the desert, the priest's heroism in death and in the visionary debate with the snake. This technique makes both Guerra's and Father Pierre's piecing together of how it happened all the more effective in coming to appreciate Father Louis's legendary status.

The landscape for Father Louis is mapped in his mind and importantly so for his life depends upon accounting for it. Its distances like his own humanity are measured in time. And his endurance is determined by the presence of water. The significance of Father Louis's journey through the desert, fighting off the hazards of nature to bring "the greatest news in all life" to his river people, is the significance of Christian humanism. His prayer when he says Mass for the Guerra family reflects this belief in man and God: "Oh, God,

Who has established the nature of man in wondrous dignity, and even more wondrously hast renewed it . . ." (*PS*, 419).

It is this prayer to which Father Louis testifies in his death at the climactic point in the story. Guerra, like Father Pierre, knows that Father Louis is too old and exhausted to continue his journey but he relents when scolded by the old priest and allows him to leave. As he heads south to San Ygnacio, Father Louis goes to his fated rendezvous with the devil in the desert. Disoriented, he rides into a swarm of cicadas which he first mistakes for a singing wind. Choosing to rest for a moment under the shade of a mesquite clump he falls asleep and is bitten on the shoulder by the snake. Eve in the Garden of Eden, Christ in the wilderness, Father Louis in the desert—the archetype is well known. And in the tradition of poetic debate where evil and good argue, Father Louis talks to his special serpent. Father Louis accepts the snake's powers of evil and its ability to assume many forms. But he never denies his own humanity.

The snake is condemned to live only on earth regardless of its assumed form, while Father Louis knows and argues that through God he can transcend the physical and the material. Speaking for himself and humanity he tells the snake: "I and my brothers, and my children, know that beyond matter lies spirit, and that it is there where answers are found . . ." (*PS*, 430). His dying words are those of the "Magnificat," spoken in Latin and reflecting a lifetime of prayer and devotion to God and his blessed handmaid, Mary. With the words of that prayer on his lips, a lowly priest in the desert at once dies and is exalted.

Horgan's stories about the European settlement of the Southwest in the early historical past portray various Catholic priests as heroic humanists struggling with their own faith and exile in a vast new-world wilderness. Their persons are transitory but their faith is not, bestowing on them a humble saintliness in their sacrifice and martyrdom. In these stories Native Americans are seldom dramatized as individuals. Horgan avoids this, choosing instead to characterize Hispanics like Guerra and the Castillo brothers. His concern is clearly with the Spanish and French colonists and not with the distant historical past before their coming. When he came to write *Great River*, however, he would reckon further with the "ancients" and the Indian Rio Grande.

Many of his other stories are about the lives that came into the Southwestern landscape in the later historical past of the Anglo-American pioneer, settler, and soldier, in that period of the nineteenth century just before what Horgan at his moment of writing in the twentieth century calls the "legendary present." Some of these stories of the later historical past now merit attention. Pioneers replace priests as the featured lives as the European wave of colonization is followed by the "American" wave. The panorama extends, the "heroic triad" of cultures remains with new forces building. And Horgan paints it grandly—across the whole sweep of the landscape.

Later historical past. This panel in Horgan's short-fiction "mural" of the Southwest concerns "westering," that heroic "theme for the American imagination, the turning of a whole national impulse westward" (*FL*, 53). The impetus for such a migration Horgan sees as both familiar and transcendent, practical and religious. He observes that by the time this national westering took place the American character had already "established its Yankeeness," so that the pioneer and Uncle Sam were images for the whole country. Like the European priests before him the pioneer was heroic in human terms: "Taken as a whole, the overland movement must remain majestic and magnificent, a moment of history that will live as a triumph of the human spirit" (*FL*, 55). With the wagon trains came the famous roads West and armies and soldiers to help the settlers. Forts, commerce, and communication grew and Santa Fe became a provincial capital. First there were the traders and trappers, then the cattle industry and the railroad—a new empire. As Horgan describes it, the "biography of that young giant who grew westward in the nineteenth century" began to take shape in the recorded memories of those who turned west (*FL*, 79). Horgan's stories contribute to that biography.

"The Captain's Watch" deals with the resolve and cooperation of the westering spirit. The action, which occurs in the 1820s, involves three men: a trader from Pennsylvania who narrates the story; a U.S. cavalry lieutenant named Stackleton; and a plains Indian called Morning Star. There are other prominent characters, especially Captain Morgan, present in memory and whose death by Indian massacre motivates a mission to secure a treaty and recover his watch and saber; and his widow, Mrs. Morgan, and son, Jem. It falls to Lieutenant Stackleton, a survivor of the massacre, to continue the captain's work of making the West secure for settlers like the narrator and their families. Ironically, the Indian appropriately named Morning Star helps show the way. Cooperation and community must win out. Soldiers, Indians, and pioneer families are reconciled.

The narrator has traveled West to Spring Willow, Missouri, leaving his wife and child in Pennsylvania, and bringing his freight wagons and supplies to the Missouri departure point, waiting for spring and the first caravan West—once Captain Morgan makes a treaty with the Indians to allow travel to Santa Fe. The narrator had made his own way to Santa Fe before and that trip convinced him that in the West was his home and his fortune. As a boarder with Mrs. Morgan, he hears Lieutenant Stackleton's story of the massacre. Responding both to the lieutenant's pleas for men to finish the mission and obtain a treaty, and to Mrs. Morgan's request to find her husband's watch and saber for Jem's sake, the narrator becomes a soldier for the two months required to travel three hundred and fifty miles west of Spring Willow and return.

When the Indians are reached a friendship is made with one who comes up to the sentries at night. The soldiers treat the Indian humanely and when he points to the morning star they give him the name of "Morgenstern" or Morning Star. It is through Morning Star that the captain's possessions are returned, for when the shaded lanterns of the troop are seen the Indians think the stars are disrupted. A peace agreement results. The Indian, partly through the similarity of sounds between his name and the captain's, points to a West of harmony with nature, of belonging—just as the captain does in his "duty" and in the letter found in the lining of his salvaged cap. In the captain's death is a legacy of the westering spirit. And the narrator returns to Spring Willow resolved to take not only his family but Mrs. Morgan and Jem futher West with him.

A story representative of the Pecos valley area in the 1880s is "The Candy Colonel." Residents of Roswell in particular find insights into their historical past here. But the themes are universal. The characters are both representative and individualized pioneers.

"The Candy Colonel" juxtaposes the present of aging Colonel Richard Fielding, as he revisits Roswell in the autumn of 1931, with his past as a young cavalry lieutenant stationed at Fort Banning in 1884. That was the year of the Brady's Mill Massacre, a year which Fielding will never forget. As he sits in front of the court house giving candy to children, Fielding is unknown as one who played a role in Roswell history and is recognized only as the "Candy Colonel" by the children. One of the Mexican-American children, Mary Melendez, awakens the colonel's memory of his love for a girl similarly named Maria Melendez, and her death in the massacre.

Seated in the town square with the little girl's eyes reflecting his past, the colonel relives how he came to know Maria's father, Patricio, fell in love with Maria, and was requested to quell the feud between the Anglo miller, Brady, and Patricio's cousin, Enrique, over Brady's exploitation of Mexican-Americans. When he sends word to Fielding for help from the soldiers, Patricio brings about his own death, shot by an angered group of his own people who have overtaken the mill. In the crossfire, Maria is killed by soldiers. Paradoxically, through the loss of Maria, Fielding comes into a closer relationship with all humanity as reflected in the prayer he senses in her death: "Man in his content shall know the memory of his evil. And in sorrow, he shall yield something of his heart to the enrichment of all life and by bearing pain he shall come to recognize only the eternal joys when they appear before him" (*FL*, 106). Horgan's fiction is filled with prayer in the face of death and crisis. Here not a priest but a soldier expresses Horgan's humanism.

As Fielding returns in awareness to the present-day Roswell of 1931 and looks ahead to his own eternity, he philosophically draws a parallel between his own past duty as a soldier, painful as it at times was, and his human duty: "And was not that duty the larger one which put us together in life than the one which put us indifferently separate in death?" (*FL*, 109). Anglo-American and Mexican-American must recognize the mutual family of man.

Legendary present. Horgan's stories of the legendary Southwestern present, the twentieth century, also slip into the historical past of the nineteenth century. The past, historical and legendary, weighs heavily on all of Horgan's fiction, just as does place—especially in the Southwest which has such a visible past. Stories like "The Candy Colonel," though predominately in the historical past of the nineteenth century, take their present in the twentieth century. On a shorter continuum, "The Surgeon and the Nun" balances early and mid-twentieth century. "The Peach Stone" is more of the twentieth century but many family ghosts of ancestry add their haunting effect.

In turning, then, from a consideration of Horgan's stories about the lives and landscapes of the historical Southwestern past to some of his stories about the legendary Southwestern present one is reminded that in Horgan's fiction past and present are not mutually exclusive. This becomes an overreaching theme in these stories.

In "The Surgeon and the Nun" the legendary present is 1935: a doctor looks back to the year 1905 and an emergency operation which, with the help of a westering nun, he performed successfully, despite dangerous and threatening conditions to himself, the nun, and their patient. The locale is the southeastern New Mexico plains near the town of Eddy. As doctor and nurse, a partnership by the chance of their both being on the same train, the surgeon and the nun fight ignorance and spite, in addition to illness, and win—bringing science and faith to a desolate region in need of both the restoration of body and spirit. Thrown together by fate and necessity, the surgeon and the nun carry out their companion duties of doing good for humankind. In accounting for their success as a team, the doctor speculates: "I think it was because both she and I, in our professions, somehow belonged to a system of life which knew men and women at their most vulnerable, at times when they came face to face with the mysteries of the body and soul, and could look no further, and needed help then" (*PS*, 273).

The surgeon's attitude toward his antagonists is impatient and, in retrospect, comic. In order to perform an appendectomy on one of the stricken gang of rail workers, who must either have the operation on the spot or die, the doctor confronts the cruelty of the foreman of the section gang and the protectiveness of the Mexican-American workers, both of whom seek to prevent the operation. The surgeon and the nun, as they carry out the operation in a shed by the railroad tracks, respect each other and if not the patient himself then something the surgeon calls "the human value," "something that has to be done for somebody else" (*PS*, 266). That value sustained the surgeon for over thirty years.

"The Peach Stone" is a solemn story—characteristic of Horgan at his best—about love and the affirmation of life in the face of tragic death. Again the lives of a family are encountered, this time as Jodey and Cleotha Powers and their son Buddy drive four hours from their rural home near Roswell to Weed, New Mexico, and Cleotha's family burial ground. In the car with them and in their thoughts is the coffined body of their two-year old daughter, accidentally killed in a tumbleweed fire near their house. Reminiscent in some ways of the death drive in *Far from Cibola*, Buddy's teacher, Miss Arlene Latcher accompanies them trying to offer solace. Essentially, the story involves the reawakening of Cleotha's belief, both in the car and at the cemetery, in life after death, a belief in the regenerative power of nature as symbolized in the game she had played as a girl which, predicated on childish faith in miracle, insisted that if one held a peach stone in their hand long enough and really believed, it would sprout. To Cleotha the peach stone "myth" of her childhood has all the meaning of a procreation parable. She says, "It seemed to me, in between my *sensible* thoughts, a thing that any woman could probably do. It seemed to me like a parable in the Bible. I could preach you a sermon about it this day" (*PS*, 344). And that is just what she does in a restoration of faith in the life force. It is Cleotha who aids Miss Latcher in her loneliness and childlessness; it is Cleotha who comforts her husband and absolves him of his feelings of guilt for having neglected to remove the tumbleweeds from a fence in the first place.

Cleotha and Arlene are a contrast in the amount of strength they marshal in the face of the child's burial. It is Arlene, the ostensible comforter, who breaks down into prolonged crying—as much for her own aloneness as for the child and parents; while Cleotha rallies and finds strength to go on, absorbing the lost life of her daughter into a consideration for the life of others. The drive and burial bring Arlene face to face with a depth of self she had heretofore refused to acknowledge in her mistaken condescension toward Cleotha, a woman she had fooled herself into thinking poor and not pretty. Her air of sympathy cannot hold, and her old soul ache enters into her consciousness and destroys her composure.

Arlene's reveries about ancient Rome and the painting of the agony of the Christian martyrs, her identification with them, underscores the human agony and triumph of the Powers family in their real and immediate consolation and love for each other. It is Cleotha's love expressed for her surviving child, Buddy, that finally breaks Miss Latcher's reverie and fanciful indulgence in distant martyrdom and brings her up short in the realization of, ironically, her envy of the Powers family in their human contact and grief: "She envied them their entanglement with one another, and the dues they paid each other in the humility of the duty they were performing on this ride, to the family burial ground at Weed" (*PS*, 355). As Arlene sobs in sorrow for herself, it is Cleotha who comforts her.

These are but a few of Horgan's short stories and novellas set in the Southwest of the historical past and the legendary present. They suggest the extent of his panoramic prose-mural of lives and landscapes across the centuries of Hispanic and Anglo-American settlement. The Southwest is only one region depicted. Stories of both coasts also play a role in his transcontinental perspective.

Stories Far West

Several of Horgan's short stories are set in California. As in his novels *Give Me Possession* (1957) and *Memories of the Future* (1966), World War II often provides a background. But the California of Hollywood and the movies is also in evidence. Generally his shorter California fiction concerns mid-twentieth-century society of the 1940s, 1950s, and 1960s. To say that Horgan's Far West fiction is war fiction is not the real point. But it was World War II which first took him to California and provided many impressions. It is a later West of California which interests him in such stories as "National Honeymoon" and "The Small Rain." His advocacy of "the human value" continues in these stories.

Horgan's best California story, "National Honeymoon" (1950), involves the public compromising of Gustavus Adolphus Earickson and his wife, Roberta May, by Hollywood showman Gail Burke—referred to satirically as "Gail Burke Himself," in all his self-embracing celebrity. Flown from New Mexico to Hollywoood and the revelations of Burke's radio program, "National Honeymoon," where newlyweds tell their story and receive wonderful prizes in return, bride and groom Earickson give away more than they get. They give away their private story and in the process are mocked by "your favorite father-in-law, Gail Burke Himself." With the prizes of car, wardrobe, diamond ring, honeymoon hotel suite, tour of the motion-picture studios, monogrammed silver, and silk sheets and furniture for their special dream room in their home—with all of this they win heartache and a sense of betrayal. Roberta May is especially affected, for she arranged the radio-show appearance in the first place, telling her husband about it only at the last minute. Furthermore, Roberta May talks more openly to Gail Burke, although sensing her betrayal of private matters—about how they met, how she fell in love, Gus's heroism in Germany during World War II, how they courted, and their quarrels over Gus's insisting that she quit her job. Gus talks too, even laughs at Burke's taunting, but it is out of a love for his wife that he shares in the betrayal.

After the show—in their gift hotel suite—Roberta May tearfully admits her mistake and asks Gus for forgiveness. Gus consoles her with a take-charge. "I'll fix everything" attitude, resolved to return all the gifts directly to Burke. Horgan is aware of the comedy implicit in the battle of wills and the ultimate male dominance in the lives of the newlyweds. He satirizes it somewhat, but approvingly. For if his couple is naive and the groom chauvenistic, they are also sincere in their answers to Burke and in their love for each other. The radio audience senses this. And the honesty of their valuing of each other, countryfied New Mexicans that they are, puts to shame the dishonesty of Burke and his show.

Human love and value in marriage and friendship supersedes all else in Horgan's California stories.

Stories Northeast

The Mid-Atlantic states of New York and Pennsylvania provide the settings for Horgan's Northeast stories. As in several of his novels, the Rochester and Buffalo of his youth turn up in the shorter fiction. And the Chadds Ford region, the Pennsylvania of the N. C. Wyeth family, is also incorporated into the locales of these stories.

One Red Rose For Christmas (1951), a novella in the tradition of *The Saint Maker's Christmas Eve*, is a representative Northeast story. Horgan's concern is with love and its gift as examples of the "humble powers" and the universal good will implicit in the story of Christmas and its spirit—and again, with new starts in life and changed outlooks. The setting is presumably Buffalo, the orphanage of Mount St. Catherine's Home for Girls "in that big city on the Great Lakes famous for its furious winters" (*HP*, 59). And the landscape, particularly when the snow finally covers it, is once more an integral part of the characters' lives.

The central ambiguity of the story, for Mother Mary Seraphim, the reverend mother and superior of Mount St. Kit's, is whether to accept in faith, as a sign that her prayer for Christmas has been answered, or to discount, as only a surprising coincidence, the gift of one red rose.

One year prior to the time of the story, Christmas past, a terrible fire destroyed part of the orphanage, and Sister St. Anne had died from exposure in the early morning while waiting outside, a guardian to the children, during the early morning hours of the fire. As a sister by blood, as well as of the faith, to Mother Seraphim, Sister St. Anne's death is doubly tragic for the reverend mother. She prays to Sister St. Anne during the Christmas of the story for one red rose, as a sign that her dear sister is in heaven "with Our Divine Lord": " 'Send me a red rose, and I will know, and I will be happy and you can pray for me' " (*HP*, 86). She does receive a rose as a gift from Kathie, the young girl who had confessed causing the fire and, indirectly, the death of Sister St. Anne. In an attempt to sort out her confused feelings, Mother Seraphim seeks the advice of the bishop who visits the orphanage on Christmas night. The bishop advises Mother Seraphim to accept the rose as a sign from heaven, and to truly love Kathie. Mother Seraphim finds Kathie sleepless that night and wishing for snow. Mother Seraphim ushers Kathie into the kitchen for a clandestine cocoa party, and, in a continuation of miracles, watches as the snow comes, changing not only the external landscape but their internal lives as well: "All the familiar ugly things of the street were turning before their very eyes into new and beautiful shapes" (*HP*, 121). In such imagery is the culmination of all the ironic coupling of beauty and ugliness, faith and doubt, truth and lies, divine and human that make up the story and emphasize the differences in perception given the varying assumptions and values by which the characters live their lives.

Horgan's transcontinental lives and landscapes as seen in his stories Southwest, Far West, and Northeast reveal aspects of common humanity. His shorter fiction, like his novels, gives a strong sense that humanity owes a special devotion through itself to God who, in the Christian account of things at least, became man and lived on Earth.

Chapter Four

History as Biography

Ralph Waldo Emerson said, "All history becomes subjective; in other words there is properly no history, only biography."[1] Such a man-centered assumption also pervades Horgan's Pulitzer-Prize-winning books of history, *Great River: The Rio Grande in North American History* (1954) and *Lamy of Santa Fe* (1975). Horgan's humanism is so strong in these works that history and place take on their meanings in persons. Horgan thus need not be regarded as either a novelist or a historian/biographer, but as a humanist author whose interest is mankind—in imagination and in fact, individually and collectively. Great men make great history as "representative men."

Although *Great River* dramatically announced Horgan to be a historian; and although it clearly began another phase of his career which saw the appearance of numerous historical and biographical works culminating, most recently, in *Lamy of Santa Fe*, he has from the beginning combined the writing of nonfiction with fiction. The seeds of his history of the Rio Grande and his biography of Archbishop Lamy are present in his earlier writings about the Southwest, notably *From the Royal City* (1936). Likewise, other lesser works like *Centuries of Santa Fe* (1956) which follow *Great River* are implicit in that masterwork. Nowhere does Horgan merely repeat himself.

Much of his biographical and even his critical writing is autobiographical in the sense that friends have received his tribute. Abraham Lincoln is of continuing interest to Horgan, as well. From the early 1930s into the 1980s, he has assumed that place, time and events—real and imagined—have meaning in and because of humanity. In this sense, as novelist and as historian he is a biographer.

Great Histories

Horgan's writing is historical in that recognizable dates, times, places, and manners provide the framework for his narratives. Some of his novels are historical in the traditional sense of actually retelling such things as Oñate's 1598 expedition into New Mexico or General Crook's soldiering in the Apache wars of the 1880s. But in the larger sense of times and ways portrayed, all of his novels and short stories are historical and "realistic." Even the fantasy which he sometimes engages in—visions and dreams of the miraculous and divine—is always grounded in an historical present. History remains important in his writing because one senses that the past shapes the present and the future, "ordains" both individual and group character. In Horgan's most recent novel, *Mexico Bay*, it is appropriate that his protagonist, Howard Debler, is once again a historian.

Just as Horgan's fiction is inherently historical, his histories, always tending toward narrative and descriptive modes, have recourse to the techniques of fiction. What he says about the history in his fiction, more explicitly the Southwest of *The Common Heart* (1942), is true about the fiction in his history: "Because the land was so vacant, and its forms so huge and abiding, it seemed that what men and women had enacted there long ago could still be seen if you looked hard enough with eyes closed. . . . And if history did not tell enough about what people did in that land, then what they did must instead be invented" (*MS*, 594). Far from suggesting that he is an inaccurate historian because of looking with eyes closed, intuitively, what this says about him is that he is (like his historian characters) more artist than scientist.

The Southwest. The table of contents of *Great River* reveals this design: "The Indian Rio Grande," "The Spanish Rio Grande," "The Mexican Rio Grande," "The United States Rio Grande." The design, later, of *The Heroic Triad* (excerpted from *Great River*) is "Indian/Rio Grande," "Latin/Conquering Spaniards & Their Mexican Sons," and "Anglo-American/Sons of Democracy." Both books begin with a prologue on place, on the "riverscape."[2] This "panoramic" structure—representing what Horgan calls the "laminated" cultures which developed in recurrent colonization along the Rio Grande—appeared as a design for his historical writing in the 1930s with "About the Southwest: A Panorama of Neuva Granada" (1933), and *New Mexico's Own Chronicle* (1937).

"About the Southwest" deals expressly with "The Heroic Triad" and the "Land." *Chronicle* is subtitled "Three Races in the Writings of Four Hundred Years." It is a natural enough design to sustain over several decades in several variations since it reflects the cultural history of the Southwest. It is essentially the same concept which Frederick Jackson Turner advanced in his thesis about "The Significance of the Frontier in American History." Horgan's Albuquerque friends, the Fergussons, adopted a similar design for their histories of the Southwest: Harvey Fergusson's *Rio Grande* (New York, 1933) and Erna Fergusson's *New Mexico: A Pageant of Three Peoples* (New York, 1951).

Horgan reviewed Harvey Fergusson's *Rio Grande* in terms that could be applied to his own essay, "About the Southwest," and his own fiction then in the making. He praised Fergusson's universal applications of Rio Grande source materials, saying, "What Mr. Fergusson does here is to make a panorama of the different sorts of life that have been in the Southwest, arranging his essays in a sequence of chronology, from the early Indians to the latest A.T. & S.F. Country Club occupation."[3] The entire review, with talk of Fergusson's "heroic landscape" and his themes of frequent change across the face of an unchanging land, preview in ironic ways, given Horgan's later book on the Rio Grande, his own method and performance.

Like Fergusson, Horgan renders the history of the Southwest from an urbane, ethnocentric Anglo-American perspective—one that implicitly views each phase of colonization, Spaniard dominating Indian, Anglo dominating Spaniard, as exemplifying the progress of Europeanized and Americanized humanistic and cultural values. In this sense, Horgan, like Turner, is writing from elitist rather than populist assumptions about progress and civilization. This is not to say that Horgan has no empathy for Native American culture. This is reflected, in part, in Horgan's friendship with Erna Fergusson and with his remarks about her own attitude toward Native Americans and Mexican Americans from which he learned much. In his introduction to a recent edition of Erna Fergusson's *New Mexico*, Horgan observes about his friend and guide into ways of regarding the triple culture of the Southwest: "She was always able to detect the common humanity as against the abstract differences imposed by nation, language, skin color, or separately derived mythology."[4]

Much the same thing might be said of Horgan as historian of the Southwest and its cultures. In all of his many books about Native Americans, Hispanics, and Anglos—their interactions and their land—a sympathetic respect is shown for common humanity and the geography of its unfolding.

New Mexico's Own Chronicle (1937) was intended as a textbook on state history when it was compiled by Maurice Garland Fulton and Horgan. The uniqueness of the volume is in its arrangement of original "own story" sources into a connected narrative of events, all told firsthand. Diaries, letters, interviews, newspaper and magazine pieces are anthologized into an autobiography of New Mexico and the heritage of its three races. The biographies of the frontiersmen—Gregg, Lamy, and Cutting—to whom the book is dedicated are only three of the many lives featured in the evolution of the character of New Mexico itself. The concern for the greatness of humanity as hero is evidenced in the stated hope that "Our chief concern has been the life of the ordinary man or woman."[5] Josiah Gregg, Archbishop Lamy, and the city of Santa Fe are prominent topics, waiting for much future elaboration by Horgan. Philip Stevenson, Santa Fe playwright and the person to whom Horgan dedicated *Far From Cibola* (1938), was one of the original compilers of the volume; and his essay on Santa Fe's changeless character also anticipates Horgan's later books on the Royal City. *Chronicle* is a significant precursor to Horgan's later, major southwestern histories just as it incorporates much of his "About the Southwest" essay, especially in the last pages entitled "The Three Southwestern Peoples."

Two other historical essays about the Southwest that bear mentioning demonstrate Horgan's continued reliance on the idea of the region's heroic triad of cultures. In 1947, shortly after Horgan left the Army, "Survey Southwest" appeared as the introduction to *Look* magazine's Southwest volume in its *Look at America* series. And in 1962 Horgan wrote yet another essay on "New Mexico," this time for the *Saturday Evening Post.*[6]

Just as *Rome Eternal* (1959) is a biographical tribute to a holy city of faith, Horgan's writings about Santa Fe serve as biographies of that holy and royal city.[7] Several of Horgan's histories, early and late, portray Santa Fe: *From the Royal City* (1936); *The Centuries of Santa Fe* (1956); *Lamy of Santa Fe* (1975); and a short introduction to Oliver La Farge's *Santa Fe* (1959).

Centuries of Santa Fe is a more complete realization of the form tentatively expressed in *From the Royal City.*[8] Both works complement each other, as well as *Great River* and *Lamy.* Both record the life in Santa Fe over three centuries by means of biographies of imaginary and real personages. Horgan as "The Chronicler" in the concluding chapter of *Centuries* writes anonymously but autobiographically about Santa Fe in the twentieth century, since his arrival in New Mexico in 1915. He cites the changes and the vestiges of previous centuries from the perspective of one who has left the city and returned, a resident and visitor over the years. The biography of place and person thus intermingle in a kind of friendship of humanity with Santa Fe across the ages—"from" and "of" the time and place and "person" that is this picturesque city of "character."

From The Royal City portrays five lives, beginning with "The Captain General" (Don Diego de Vargas) in 1690, and ending with "Frock Coats & the Law," an account of Governor Lew Wallace in 1878. In between are, first, a character sketch of a distraught Spanish aristocrat and his mother who comes to Santa Fe in 1730 to "rescue" her wayward soldier son from the city's temptation to sin; next, the arrival in 1780 of the bishop of Durango and the duel of minds involved in his subjugation of the Franciscans; then, the political and familial delights of the merchant Levi Wurzburg upon General Kearny's occupation of the city in 1846. These character sketches involve the adjustments of newcomers who as exiles in a strange land must find and match their characters in community, order, and settlement.

Similiarly, in *Centuries*, even the great and famous historical characters are presented more or less anonymously. Josiah Gregg, although not mentioned by name, is identifiable as "The Missouri Trader: 1821." Jean Baptiste Lamy makes his appearance in several of the ten biographies. Archaeologist Adolph Bandelier's nineteenth-century presence in Santa Fe makes up a large portion of "The Doctor of Medicine: 1883." Lew Wallace, Billy the Kid, and the Lincoln County War; General Stephen Watts Kearny and his peaceful conquest of Santa Fe in 1846; the breaking away of Mexico from Spanish dominion in 1825; the various phases and persons involved in the Spanish colonization of New Mexico—priests, soldiers, and settlers, all are portrayed not as events and names but as human history. Each life, real and imaginary, faces its time in Santa Fe with its own individual sense of duty.

Such illustrious Westerners as Walter Prescott Webb and Oliver La Farge, in their reviews of *Centuries*, were not convinced that Horgan's method of mixing fact and fiction was a success. Webb suggested that the book came closer to "the impression of costume jewelry" than the purer "gold of literature" or the "silver of history." Moreover, he felt frustrated by Horgan's keeping his protagonists anonymous.[9] La Farge felt that the characters at times "become no more than mediums for telling about real personages and at moments that telling, indirect and too concise, slows to a walk."[10]

For Webb to be lost and disappointed in Horgan's method is surprising. La Farge's feeling that Horgan's anonymous lives are merely props for presenting the "real" historical personages who appear, seems equally to miss the point. Implicit throughout the histories is the idea of the ordinary greatness in humanity, both famous and anonymous.

The Rio Grande. The naturalness of Horgan's triadic design for his histories and for the revelation of them as biography of person and place, finds a related but larger and more panoramic metaphor than the city of Santa Fe across the centuries. That metaphor is the Rio Grande. The phrase "great river" is not just the title of one of Horgan's major historical works, but is a phrase that appears throughout his Southwestern writings. And it is the biography of that place in the largest sense that his novels and histories record.

From his earliest *Southwest Review* essay in 1933, Horgan seems destined to write *Great River* (1954). It is a synthesis of his historical writings (and in some ways his fiction too), through the 1930s and 1940s. Works like *The Centuries of Santa Fe, Conquistadors in North American History*, even *Lamy of Santa Fe*—all published after *Great River*—are derivative from that work.

Just how significant *Great River* is in Horgan's career as an artist is seen in a letter (a copy of which is in Horgan's possession) written to the Honorable Hugh M. Milton II, then assistant secretary of the army at the time Horgan had finished the book and was reading galleys. General Milton had requested that Horgan consider returning to active duty under him in Washington. In a long and gracious letter of respect and regret, dated 12 May 1954, Horgan demurs:

> Do you see how wholly I am oriented toward my writing and its associated preoccupations, including a kind of life, spiritual and intellectual and even social, that makes production of my work possible? All of this represents the essential me. I put it all aside during my Army service. This took the most grim and incessant self-discipline. Now I have spent years since the war learning to be an artist again. I begin to feel that I am managing it.

Horgan had consciously decided by 1940 to write a book on the Rio Grande. He worked on it in earnest after the war for eight years from 1946 until 1954—traveling the river's 1800 miles three times; making dozens of shorter trips; painting as well as writing his field notes. After *Great River* he was doubly convinced that he was a writer above all else.[11]

Most reviewers were impressed by Horgan's scholarship and method in *Great River*. D. W. Brogan called it "one of the most fascinating books in recent American historiography" and praised Horgan as a novelist-historian who "reads more into faces and voices than a pedantic academic historian would willingly do."[12] Milton S. Byam called it "a monument to diligent, painstaking research that is as interesting as it is definitive."[13] *Time* magazine said, "*Great River* is not only a fine job of historical research. It fuses the imagination of a good novelist . . . with a remarkable sense of the region's character."[14] La Farge called it "close to being monumental," leaving Horgan "with a definite standing as an historian and with his status as a writer enhanced."[15] J. Frank Dobie hailed Horgan as an artist, "a master of proportions, perspective and details," adding, "His book is an unfoldment of life with stretches of narrative as vivid as 'Livy's pictured page' and essays as bold as the divagations of Henry Fielding."[16] Walter Prescott Webb offered this evaluation: "I would not say in public that he has turned out the most comprehensive and adequate history of an American river, but I will say that his is as good as the best."[17] Apparently the Carnegie Corporation thought so too because in 1957 *Great River* was selected as one of 350 books to act as American ambassadors abroad.

Even so, amid all of its honors and praise, *Great River* had an ambivalent if not controversial reception as "history." Stanley Walker, in an unfavorable review, posed the question, "Pretty, but is it history?" He objected to Horgan's style, calling it confusing and embarrassing in its "occasional lofty pretentiousness"—part of something he names "New Mexico baroque."[18] Frank D. Reeve, in an even more disparaging essay-review, answered Walker by saying "It is sometimes pretty, but it is not good history."[19] La Farge, Dobie, and Webb also objected to aspects of Horgan's historiography. La Farge viewed Horgan as an amateur historian, most notably in his neglect of French expeditions through Texas that originated in Santa Fe and St. Louis; his failure to realize that the Pueblo Indians were not a single cultural unit; his treating them as "faceless men"; and his being "excessively soft on the Catholic Church."[20] Dobie objected to Horgan's idolizing the Spanish over the Indians' conformity to the point that "He barely touches on the Inquisition that reduced Spanish intellect to the same conformity and killed Spanish power."[21] Webb complained, "As a historian I am a little vexed that he has made the sources difficult to find by putting notes at the end of the book and by foregoing all use of reference figures in the text."[22] Erna Fergusson thought *Great River* magnificent in its descriptions; however, she wished Horgan had not seemed so much on the side of the Spanish and the U.S. Army.[23]

Great River's faults are minor in the face of the magnitude of the overall effort. Most of the criticism fails to consider the whole. This is regrettable in that what Horgan attempts is a sweeping picture of the land, lives, and times of the Rio Grande—a chronology of social, political, and geographical history and story.

What *Great River* amounts to is history as biography—the biography of the river, of Native American life five or so centuries before the discovery of that river by the Spanish and of the Anglo-American pioneers who came later; "biography" from before European time through the mid-twentieth-century technology of Los Alamos and the atom bomb. The assumptions which underlie the telling of the life of the river and the lives which came to it are humanistic. The book values all human life and its uses of nature, but it champions the stage by stage change which came to the river in terms of "progress," of the implantation of European and Anglo-American civilization. The laminations of culture which have taken place there, the "recurrent frontiers" represent not just change but improvement. In this scheme each culture's energy was both stronger and somehow better in allowing it to prevail—culminating in the "individualism" and democracy of the Anglo-American settlers. Horgan writes,

> The Indian society had always been arrested in an anonymous communal arrangement by the absence of the idea of the individual. The Spanish society was built on an inertia which allowed the high cultivation of the individual yet denied it any expression that was not in harmony with the prevailing official position of the state. Now imagining new experience until it occurred, the American settlers brought a frame of life in which the individual was not only permitted but obliged to create himself socially. (*GR*, 620)

The biographies of the individuals Horgan portrays, their type of character in coming to the river over the centuries are too numerous to list here in any kind of detail. There are soldiers, priests, governors, explorers, mountain men, traders, cowboys, presidents, the famous and anonymous. They are all filled with a sense of exile, challenge, enthusiasm, and wonder. Their motives are as various as their lives and occupations. They are, however, presented as trying to come to a new sense of their own character in relation to that of the river and to the mixed cultural heritage of that place.

It is a story of travel and possession, of shifting boundaries of identity and ownership. In book 2 it is the biography of exploration and conquest of the Conquistadors for honor, Christ, and king; and of the Franciscans who in the first quarter of the seventeenth century built more than fifty churches. The Battle of Acoma is told—and the Pueblo Indian revolt of 1680 led by Popé, a San Juan Indian. For a time that rebellion marked the end of the Spanish empire in New Mexico—until 1692 when Popé's federation of pueblos broke up and Diego José de Vargas reconquered New Mexico under the banner of the Blessed Virgin, La Conquistadora.

After the reconquest of New Mexico by Vargas, Santa Fe lapsed into a neglected northern river kingdom. In 1747 Spanish power still controlled all of the lower Rio Grande, including colonial Texas, but excluding the source waters of what is now Colorado. But from the East, American sovereignty began to intrude. Spain gave Louisiana back to France and in 1802 the French claimed the Rio Grande as the western boundary to Louisiana—only to sell all of whatever was Louisiana to the United States. President Jefferson thought the Rio Grande to be Louisiana's boundary too.

While Spain and the United States disputed boundaries, in 1805 Kentuckian James Pursley became the first U.S. citizen to enter Santa Fe from the north for purposes of commerce. In 1806 U.S. troops moved into disputed territory along the Rio Grande and Lieutenant Zebulon Pike was dispatched into New Mexico. Much attention is devoted to Pike's captivity and forced march under guard down the river to Chihuahua and eventual expulsion from New Spain. Horgan portrays Pike as a significant early historian of the Spanish west. With Pike the source waters of the Rio Grande entered American history.

Book 3 follows the history of the Rio Grande into the twentieth century as Mexico and the U.S. were drawn toward the Mexican War.

Colonel Stephen F. Austin's settlement of Texas; Benjamin Edwards's founding of Fredonia, the short-lived Texas republic; the opening of the Santa Fe Trail for commerce with Mexico in 1824; Santa Anna's rise from general to president of Mexico and the events leading to the Mexican march on San Antonio and the Alamo in 1835 and 1836—these are some of the salient events and personages Horgan follows in his account of the Mexican Rio Grande.

All of Horgan's battle scenes are done in sobering detail. But nowhere in *Great River* is he more brilliantly artful than in his accounts of the Alamo and Goliad, making them with their dead—slain in battle and executed by the hundreds—vividly meaningful in terms of the human courage and sorrow behind the Texan battle cry, "Remember the Alamo! Remember Goliad!" In Horgan's account, Houston's surprise routing of Santa Anna at San Jacinto Creek on 21 April 1836 could make a Texas patriot out of the most revengeless reader. Horgan's use of dialogue in bringing fugitive Santa Anna before a heroic Sam Houston arranging for the national independence of Texas brings final irony to the chapter title, "From Mexico's Point of View." The full force and motive of the Texas victory is made clear: "Within Texas, the Mexican point of view ceased to be significant" (*GR*, 541).

The Texas victory meant more conflict about the Rio Grande boundary. The Texas Republic laid claim to all the Rio Grande as the western boundary of Texas—including all of New Mexico east of the river. New Mexico's Governor Manuel Armijo took xenophobic precautions against all expeditions of approaching Texans and against American merchants. Horgan softens nothing in his descriptions of Armijo's violently repulsive treatment of intruders into his territory. For one thing, Armijo decorated his executive office with scalps and ears from "enemies of the state" (*GR*, 574). And no one in the annals of Rio Grande history, at least in Horgan's version, surpasses the villainy of Captain Damasio Salazar, who commanded a brutal march down the river to Mexico City, ushering Texas Colonel Cooke's and George Wilkins Kendall's party into captivity and death.

Texan insistence on slavery hindered annexation to the United States. Abolitionists obviously opposed any attempts at annexation. Mexico too opposed it. But rather than slavery or Mexico, it was Great Britain's new friendship with Texas which hastened the issue of annexation to its resolution. In 1844 Texas became a territory of the United States. And with the election of President Polk and Texas entry into the Union in 1845, all boundary disputes became the business of the United States. Enter General Zachary Taylor and Lieutenant U. S. Grant, General Winfield Scott and Captain Robert E. Lee. Enter the Mexican War.

Book 4, "The United States Rio Grande," is concerned primarily with three events and the lives involved in them: the Mexican War; the Civil War; and Pancho Villa's raid on Columbus, New Mexico, and General John J. Pershing's punitive expedition into Mexico.

To Horgan, General Taylor's army on the north bank of the Rio Grande in 1846 represented the third culture to come to the river—the Americans, "with an energy and a complexity unknown in the earlier societies of the Indian, the Spaniard and the Mexican" (*GR*, 619). Several individuals within this new wave of "democratic man" come to the forefront; and to follow their lives is to follow the events which shaped them and which their characters shaped.

General Taylor is portrayed as "honest and good as anybody," without sophistication in dress or speech or strategy but with "a certain bull-headed obstinacy in his character [which] gave him the force . . . he could throw into a fight" (*GR*, 666). Determined to stay, as ordered, and occupy the country up to the left bank of the river, Taylor settled patiently into Fort Texas near Matamoros. The Mexicans were the first to cross the river. Taylor went to meet the enemy at Point Isabel but the Mexican attack came at Fort Texas. Battle by battle Horgan details the course of the war: the heroism and death of Major Jacob Brown in his command of Fort Texas during its shelling; Palo Alto and Resaca del la Palma where Taylor's victory scored 2,000 enemy and less than fifty Americans killed or wounded; President Polk's declaration of war against Mexico and the pincers movement that involved General Kearny's march into New Mexico and on to California; the hoopla in the East of mobilization for the war; and Taylor's rise to national hero and president.

Always one of Horgan's favorite subjects, Kearny's invasion of New Mexico is the highlight of the chapters on the Mexican War. Governor Armijo, aware of Kearny's coming and resigned to defeat, did little to rally his New Mexicans to defense. Kearny's emissary, James Magoffin, succeeded in quieting those who wanted to fight, especially Colonel Diego Archuleta. He then allied numerous wealthy and leading citizens of Santa Fe to Kearny. Governor Armijo's half-hearted defenses were meant merely to impress the Mexican government and Kearny took "bloodless possession" of Santa Fe. Very much a humanist soldier, Kearny's time in New Mexico, in Horgan's life sketch, is more social than military. With Kearny's proclamation on 22 August 1846 that the territory on both sides of the river was henceforth New Mexico Territory and part of the U.S., the debated issue that Texas's boundary extended to the east bank of the river was decided. Before Kearny turned West toward the Pacific, news reached him via Kit Carson that California was now also a U.S. territory, the battle there also won. President Polk's pincers strategy was accomplished.

But bloodier battles remained in the war with Mexico. Kearny had ordered Colonel Alexander Doniphan and his Missouri volunteers to march south to Chihuahua and join General John E. Wool's army. And, with time out to subdue marauding Navajos, he went. Fighting off a force of eleven hundred men at Brazito, Doniphan proceeded through El Paso without resistance. Reports told him that General Wool was nowhere near Chihuahua. And after some weeks of hesitation he decided to proceed if heavy guns could be sent to him from Santa Fe. Worth and his troops were assigned to General Scott for his planned invasion on the coast. Scott also called for much of Taylor's inland force, and Taylor's reaction was petulant in the face of Santa Anna's massing of troops below him at Saltillo. Before Scott could have his way, Taylor engaged Santa Anna at the Battle of Buena Vista and in two days won northern Mexico and secured the presidency. Days later Scott landed at Vera Cruz and followed the path of Cortés to Mexico City. It was the end of the Mexican War. Horgan's interest in the Mexican War is made clear also in *Mexico Bay* where his historian hero devotes years of research in a labor of love culminating in the recording, in a distinguished history, of its personages and events.

The Treaty of Guadalupe Hidalgo, signed 2 February and ratified 10 March 1848, established the Rio Grande as the boundary of the United States "from the mouth to the thirty-second parallel, and thence west to the Pacific" (*GR*, 779). For fifteen million dollars the United States acquired New Mexico (including Arizona) and California. The boundaries for America's continental destiny were drawn at long last. With the Compromise of 1850 (in which Texas, for ten million dollars, relinquished boundary claims on New Mexico land east of the Rio Grande), and with the Gadsen Treaty of 1853 (another ten million paid to Mexico for new lands in southern New Mexico and Arizona), boundaries along the Rio Grande were fixed.

Horgan next considers the history of the Rio Grande during the Civil War. Boundaries were in question again—many of the same claims, but in different terms. Confederate forces marched on the Union forces of New Mexico. Seeking to reach the gold fields of Colorado and California, and all the resources of the West for their own uses, Lieutenant Colonel John R. Baylor led the assault up the Rio Grande, proclaiming "southern New Mexico and all of Arizona as a Territory of the Confederate States, with Mesilla as its capital and himself as its military governor" (*GR*, 823). Confederate Brigadier General Henry H. Sibley and a force of 3,500 men followed Baylor's entry force. Union Colonel Edward R. S. Canby and his army of New Mexico and Colorado volunteers met Sibley near Fort Craig at the battle of Valverde on 21 February 1862. Sibley's Confederates, under the command of Colonel Tom Green, won the day. Canby's army, "in entire defeat," retreated upriver to Fort Craig and Sibley set his sights on Fort Union. Sibley took Albuquerque and Santa Fe with no difficulty. Reinforced by volunteers of the First Colorado under command of a preacher, Major John M. Chivington, the Union army on 26 and 28 March won battles east of Santa Fe in Apache Canyon and at Glorieta Pass. On 12 April Sibley retreated from Santa Fe back down the river only to encounter Colonel Canby's army at Peralta, near Los Lunas, on 15 April. Canby pursued Sibley down opposite sides of the river until Sibley left the river and turned west into the rugged San Mateo Mountains—lucky to be alive and cursing the godforsaken river country in reports to the Confederate government.

Horgan's final phase of river history is a forty-page narration dealing with revolution in twentieth-century Mexico which, as far as American involvement was concerned, was as much a military rehearsal for World War I as the Mexican War was in preparing officers for the Civil War. General Pershing's encounter with Pancho Villa brought to the great river the intrigues of German espionage, a fledgling U.S. Air Corps, and rumors of the Great War.

President Wilson's altruism met only force—in Mexico and in Europe. Horgan's portrait of Wilson points toward both his strength of character and his vulnerability. When a German ship with munitions for the Mexicans arrived at Vera Cruz on 21 April 1914, Wilson without equivocation issued orders to "Take Vera Cruz at once." Pershing, successful in the Philippines and distinguished for experience with guerrilla fighting, was ordered to Fort Bliss and all the garrisons on the border were strengthened as the provocations grew. Pershing represented the ideal man for the job: "He was himself a superb model of a soldier" (*GR*, 920). Listing his attributes as a man and a soldier—which included clear thinking and writing—Horgan augments the human side of Pershing by relating the personal tragedy under which he continued to carry out his duties. Pershing's wife and three daughters were killed in a fire at their home in San Francisco and the sad news had come to him by telephone. The entire Mexican campaign, frustrating as it was, served to steel Pershing and "his citizen army" for World War I when he would become the supreme commander of U.S. forces in Europe.

Villa's 1916 raid on Columbus, New Mexico, which prompted Wilson to order Pershing and 15,000 men to cross the border in "punitive pursuit," is described in all its early morning chaos. Some doubt exists about Villa's actual presence in the 9 March raid. But Horgan builds a case for Villa leading the attack on the evidence of Maud Wright who, as a captive, overheard plans for the raid and from a ditch on the outside of town saw Villa retreat. Villa's presence is reflected too in residents reporting that in the darkness they "thought they heard General Pancho Villa's voice 'everywhere' " (*GR*, 925). Nine citizens of Columbus were killed along with eight U.S. soldiers. Several dozens of the Villistas were killed the next day along the border. American newspapers and public opinion cried out for Villa's skin, and on 15 March Pershing crossed the border.

Through the spring and early summer, Pershing's men searched for Villa, contending with the taunts of President Carranza's forces, political haggling about the Mexican government's authorization of Pershing's crossing, and the extremes of weather, terrain, and distance. On 16 June Pershing withdrew to a holding position a hundred or so miles south of the border. By 5 February 1917 he was out of Mexico without Villa but with some satisfaction that his mission had been a success. The bandits had been scattered and "the people of northern Mexico had been taught a salutary lesson . . ." (*GR*, 934). Two months later, after much more provocation—including the infamous Zimmermann telegram which delineated ways Germany hoped to ally itself with Mexico undermining the Monroe Doctrine—Wilson declared that a state of war existed between America and Germany. German saboteurs were anticipated along the Rio Grande. The modern world, its wars and technology, had invaded the river kingdom.

Los Alamos and the atomic bomb soon appeared in a land of cliff dwellings and arrowheads.

World War II brings Horgan full circle in a personal sense. He began writing *Great River* before the war (1940–42), and resumed his writing after (1946–54). He ends his history somewhat like Henry Adams contemplating the great dynamos at the Paris exposition of 1900 and wondering where "in the Hell they are going" (*GR*, 944). But Horgan is hopeful in his "vision" of the Rio Grande and the larger world's future. Underlying his faith in "the American knack for utility" is the humanistic hope to which his entire career as a man of letters gives testament: "Among the implications of all new technics of communication and energy was the moral imperative to use them to serve rather than to destroy human society. . . . to make a neighborhood of the world" (*GR*, 945).

Great Biographies

Just as Horgan's historical writings tend to feature biography, his biographies reflect the larger history, life, and times of his subject. Lives are lived and told not just for their intrinsic value but for a larger human value as well. If the frontiers of the West reoccur, so do the biographical frontiers in all of us—those frontiers of making and remaking our lives. As humanist/artist Horgan is fascinated with the common heart as well as the individual heart. History as biography and biography as history thus converge in his writings.

Horgan's theory of biography is not so explicit that it can be reduced to formula. But he has talked about biographical writing; and the comments of his friend and fellow biographer Leon Edel are significant. Edel thinks that *Lamy* is "one of the great American biographies of all times," and was quoted in these and other words of praise in the book's promotion. In addition, Edel appreciates the novelist in Horgan when he comes to write biography, saying, "I think I value his biographical work for its delicate landscapes and his ability to read himself, through the mere 'facts,' into the emotions of his subject."[24] Edel gave Horgan advice about the writing of *Lamy* which emphasized the novelist's "rare gift" in life writing: "Write Lamy as if he were a subject of a novel. And write in the only way you can—as a novelist. It will then end by being a great Biography."[25]

As a recent symposium on biography, sponsored by the National

Portrait Gallery in Washington, attests, there are almost as many ways of telling lives as there are lives to tell. Some biographers, led by masters of the form like Edel, prefer to get at the figure "beneath the carpet," to unravel the hidden personal myths of their subjects. Other equally fine biographers, represented by Barbara Tuchman, are not as much concerned with the individual as with their subject's times—life writing as a reflection of a larger history.[26] Horgan's approach to the biographer's art is closer to the approach represented in this symposium by Tuchman than to Edel's approach.

Horgan says about his own approach to biography: "In terms of writing biography . . . the intuition of the artist is much more important than any fixed theory of how to treat a character. The strict facts and the strict information will give you keys to that intuition for biographical purpose" (H–1). Horgan does not regard his biographical writing as novelistic in any pure sense, although he does hold out for intuition's play upon fact. This play of intuition upon fact is evidenced in Horgan's biographies of presidents, traders, and priests—humanists all in their way.

Mr. President. Much of Horgan's biographical writings involve American presidents. Woodrow Wilson is one of his favorite presidents, as *Great River* and *The Thin Mountain Air* demonstrate. However, Abraham Lincoln receives the most attention—in a straight biography of Lincoln's early adulthood (*Citizen of New Salem* ([1961]); in a volume of elegiac poems (*Songs After Lincoln* [1965]); in a drama about Lincoln's Assassination (*Death, Mr. President* [1937–39, 1943); and in a related way, in *A Distant Trumpet* (1960).

George Washington, too, is the subject of a short but significant biography by Horgan; and it is with this early 1930s work that one needs to begin in looking at Horgan's fascination with presidents. In "George Washington" (1936), Horgan pictures the weekend of Washington's illness with pneumonia at Mount Vernon from the time he returned home, wet and chilled, on 12 December 1799 to his death on 14 December. It is a prose version of the numerous engravings which recorded Washington's deathbed scene. From that scene Horgan projects the course of Washington's "bequest" to Americans and his "transfiguration" to national greatness and legendary heroism. It is the man behind the symbol, and how he became a symbol, that Horgan wants to explain. In Horgan's portrait, Washington the man is unselfish, considerate, and civil. Suffering man's indignity in death,

Washington nevertheless acknowledges the mutual debt humankind owes each other. As for his bequest, it is a combination of the man, the place and the moment. Horgan says, "George Washington's life experience was anyone's, each of ours, really . . . as we each are the race in the singular, repeating in the biological and spiritual miniature of a life the immense experience of the race, so was he the American, the citizen as the microcosm of his nation."[27] It is this bequest of meeting the crisis, of citizen as microcosm of his nation that one senses in Horgan's biographical writings about Lincoln.

Horgan's three works on Lincoln combine to offer a before, during, and after portrait of the man and the President. As in his writing on Washington, Horgan attempts to portray Lincoln's essential character at his own moment in time, and his bequest to the nation of the values on which he acted. In varying forms of narrative, drama, and poetry Lincoln's life unfolds in deed and memory.

Citizen of New Salem was written in honor of the centennial of Lincoln's first inauguration on 4 March 1861. Paul Engle thought the book "as active and lively a presentation of the young Lincoln as exists."[28] While not mentioning Lincoln by name, Horgan follows him from 1830 to 1837, through his formative years in New Salem, Illinois, to his arrival in Springfield. Anticipating the fame that would be his fate in the grand anonymity of "Mr. President," and utilizing italicized bits of Lincoln's own words, Horgan presents Lincoln as a flatboatman, store clerk, candidate, militia captain, storekeeper, postmaster, scholar, legal clerk, deputy surveyor, assemblyman, and lawyer. Reinforcing the idea that Lincoln's character was affected by his place and time, Horgan provides in as few as ninety pages an amazing amount of social history and Sangamon riverscape ambiance. He calls his book an "essay in biography."[29] But it can also be read as travelogue, memoir, and regional history of central Illinois. Lincoln's character, his good humor, his physical strength, his honesty and ambition, his love of people, knowledge, and truth are the heart of the book. Citizenship shines golden in varying humanistic as well as political ways for Horgan's Lincoln. To be known as a "citizen" of New Salem and America was something Lincoln respected and prized.

Death, Mr. President was performed by the Actors' Equity and Dramatists' Guild in the Experimental Theatre in two performances in July 1942 at the Shubert Theatre in New York City. Brock Pemberton produced the play with Vincent Price in the starring role. Price recalls, "I played Mr. L. with the high Midwest voice he had but not being Raymond Massey (said one critic) I didn't have a chance. The play, I felt, had a much too short a go at it—it's extremely good, timeless and exciting."[30] Horgan says in a note to the play that Otto Eisenschiml's *Why Was Lincoln Murdered* "touched off [his] desire to write about Lincoln," and that although the play is true to history, "all the conversations have been invented, and the dramatic issues necessarily simplified."[31]

Death, Mr. President takes place in Washington, D.C., during the last three weeks of Lincoln's life in March and April 1865. The play has three acts and the cast of characters includes Lincoln, his wife, Mary, his son, Tad; his bodyguard W. H. Crook; Secretary of War Edwin M. Stanton and three senators conspiring against Lincoln's wish to end the war as fast and fairly as possible; Lieutenant General Grant and Major General Sherman; John Wilkes Booth and several of his followers; several Union guards, aides, and soldiers—most especially Private Johnnie Roundhill and his father, and Charlie Putnam and his mother Mrs. Gideon Putnam. Last, the poet Walt Whitman frames the action as both a participant and an observer, a choral voice lamenting death and divisiveness and representing the democratic brotherhood of man.

Songs After Lincoln, a collection of thirty-one poems accompanied by notes and comments and written at different times, sustains this elegiac tribute to the nation's "first Martyr Chief." The volume was published as part of the one hundredth anniversary of Lincoln's death. Lincoln's martyrdom reached across the years to touch young Horgan at the age of ten in a personal way when he would go to the Buffalo Historical Society's museum and stand before the catafalque where Lincoln's coffin once rested. That tangible object had its lifelong effect. Horgan explains, "I think that the childhood impression created in me by that piece of funerary furniture gave me a sense of Abraham Lincoln's reality, and set going for me a lifelong interest in and response to his history and its period."[32]

Matthew Hazard in *A Distant Trumpet* is the most obvious of Horgan's fictive counterparts to live out that impressionability with Lincoln and at least two of Horgan's poems in *Songs* are also incorporated in that novel: number 21, the ballad "Father Abraham and the Recruit"; and number 23, a lyric narrative, "The Schoolboy," out of which grew the opening episodes of the novel.

Grouped under headings of "The War," "The Casualty," and "The

President," Horgan's verse has the simplicity of ballads composed by the soldier and citizen voices through which Horgan speaks. Most reviewers felt the songs were too simple. DeWitt Bell thought Horgan's notes more interesting than the poems, compared the poems to "transplanted 'Shropshire Lad,' " and reduced the book to "nice rhymes for junior-high schools across the country."[33] Winfield Townley Scott said of Horgan, "His balladlike verses make their effect not so much individually but as a totality of Civil War and Lincolnian atmosphere."[34]

The verse in *Songs* is suited for much beyond adolescent literature, though Scott's point is well taken. There is a cumulative quality to the poems—and the entire book should be read in connection with Horgan's other works about Lincoln. "Biography," a condensation of *A Citizen of New Salem* and *Death, Mr. President*, follows Lincoln in colloquy form from boyhood through assassination.

Gregg and Lamy. The two lives which dominate Horgan's biographical writings are Josiah Gregg, author of *Commerce of the Prairies* (1844), and Jean Baptiste Lamy, first archbishop of Santa Fe. These two lives represent much of Horgan's humanist ideal, much of his conception about the meaning of the American West. They represent the models for the various plainsmen and priest figures, the civilizers exiled in the wilderness West, that fill Horgan's fiction. Subjects of their separate biographies, Gregg and Lamy also make their appearances in others of Horgan's historical writings. Moreover, they represent biographical and historical counterparts to Horgan's own life experience as a civilizer simultaneously alienated and absorbed by the West. In a special sense, their life experiences, their "myths" are Horgan's own.

Horgan wrote his first biographical essays about Gregg in 1941. At that time he began a long two-part biography entitled "Josiah Gregg Himself" to serve as an introduction to Maurice Garland Fulton's edition of the *Diary and Letters of Josiah Gregg.* The first of Fulton's volumes, *Southwestern Enterprises, 1840–1847*, was published in 1941; the second volume, entitled *Excursions in Mexico & California, 1847–1850*, appeared in 1944. Although the diary and letters deal with a ten-year period of trading and exploring in the West, Horgan's biographical essay covers Gregg's entire life. In 1941 Horgan also published an essay in the *Southwest Review* entitled "The Prairies Revisited: A Re-estimation of Josiah Gregg," a close look at Gregg's *Commerce of the Prairies.* In 1979 Horgan reworked these essays, wrote a new introductory essay, and published them as *Josiah Gregg and His Vision of the Early West.*[35]

Out of Gregg's log of his prairie experiences and observations Horgan turned autobiography into biography. Incorporating "Josiah Gregg, Himself" and "The Prairies Revisited" into one volume is a natural synthesis, but it raised the question of unity among some reviewers.

One reviewer chose to see *Josiah Gregg* as "a vignette of early American history" in twenty-seven essays under four headings.[36] Another reviewer called *Gregg* "biography by assertion" and asserted that statements about Gregg's character and "vision" remained unsubstantiated and short on substance: "Only a tantalizing whiff of the flavor of real life in the early West emerges."[37] William McDonald, who was not bothered by numerous divisions in format and generalizations, said, "This slim volume of fascinating essays adds life and color to our understanding of . . . the Southwest."[38]

Horgan begins with a larger biographical consideration than just Gregg—for he was part of a larger biographical pursuit, that of finding and knowing the character of the West of his time. As such, Horgan thinks of Gregg as the West's autobiographer. Others had "chased that vanishing phantom land" toward the Pacific, seeing the West as both romance and fact. Gregg sought the West in fact and shared his information in a guidebook for others in the early 1840s—before the 1849 travel guides to California gold.

On a bleak expedition along the Trinity River searching for a way over the coastal ranges to what is now Humbolt Bay, Gregg, weak from hunger, fell off his horse and died. His companions buried him somewhere near Clear Lake, California, in February 1850. He was forty-four. Within his lifetime America reached across the continent. Calling Gregg "the intellectual frontiersman of the natural world," Horgan says about Gregg's life: "His story is part of a great conquest, in which his particular weapons were curiosity and a batch of little bound books with blank pages, waiting to be written upon" (*JG*, 110).

Lamy of Santa Fe (1975) is another history Horgan was fated to write. Like *Great River* it was a book long in the making; in a sense, it originated with Horgan's move to New Mexico and first visit to Santa Fe. The biographical presence of Jean Baptiste Lamy is very much a part of Horgan's life history as person and writer. More than with Josiah Gregg there is an affinity between Lamy's journey to Santa Fe, his mission as a spiritual and cultural gardener in the wilderness, and Horgan's move West. Horgan tells about the identification process, his "following" of Archbishop Lamy in two autobiographical essays which in their titles imply the life journey toward Lamy and his biography which Horgan undertook as a man and writer: "In Search of the Archbishop" (1961) and "Convergences Toward a Biography" (1970).[39]

In his convergence with Lamy, Horgan saw Willa Cather, and not only in the pages of *Death Comes for the Archbishop.* He interrupted Cather one morning on a porch of the La Fonda Hotel in the midst of, he assumes, work on her Lamy book. Horgàn tells of this meeting with some degree of fanciful invention and with the memory of an event that had in its surprise the impact and irony of a kind of literary laying on of hands. His meeting with Cather, amounting to not much more than a bothered stare from the famous novelist, took place in 1926, a year before the publication of her story about Lamy (Cather calls him Archbishop Latour). Already a fan of Cather's at the time, Horgan had first heard of her from her sister, Elsie, who was his freshman English teacher at Albuquerque High School. Thus, some of Horgan's coming to write *Lamy* involves Willa Cather and her biographical novel which anticipated Horgan's biography of the famous churchman.[40] *Lamy*, like *Great River* two decades before it, won the Pulitzer Prize for history in 1976. But few would argue that Lamy is not a biography. There is little to be gained in quibbling over Pulitzer Prize categories; nevertheless, for *Lamy* to win in the history category demonstrates in an obvious way that as a historian Horgan is a biographer. Ultimately, what such classifying leads to is the attitude expressed by Cather who, in a reply to questions about whether her book about Lamy was history or biography or fiction, said, "Why bother?"[41] Cather's explanation of how she came to write her book on Lamy is the essay equivalent of Horgan's "In Search of the Archbishop." Naturally enough, Cather's biographical novel and Horgan's historical biography invite comparisons. And many of the reviewers of *Lamy* had Cather's work on their mind in their assessment of Horgan's book. After a point, such comparisons are irrelevant; however, they must be acknowledged.

One reviewer stated the obvious by suggesting that since Cather was not holding herself to facts, many of the incidents in her narrative are not in Horgan's.[42] Another reviewer held that although *Lamy* separates fact from legend, it is Horgan's "inspired innovations," his "improvisations," that resulted in "a novel biography just as Cather's was a biographical novel. . . ."[43] *Time*'s reviewer said that no stranger fiction could match the fact of the incongruity involved in Lamy in the deserts of the Southwest and that if Cather's success is due to her art, Horgan's "triumph is due as much to a sense of place as to a discernment of character."[44] Stressing Horgan's restoration of Lamy's life but with Cather's book in the background, F. D. Reeve said that Horgan's Lamy is a comment on Cather's Latour in the same way that the features of the Southwestern landscape comment on each other.[45] Edmund Fuller saw Cather's and Horgan's books as companion volumes and said, "Cather is worth rereading, before or after Mr. Horgan's biography."[46]

To understand the life and times of Lamy as Horgan presents them is to understand the patience and strength of an outsider in the face of the resistance of insiders toward new and unyielding leadership. Horgan does not present this conflict in terms of regrettable religious and cultural European colonization. He presents Lamy as a good and courageous man of ordinary greatness whose mission was to improve conditions in the places he was assigned and in the people he found there—to bring discipline, authority, and "civilization" to the Southwest.

In Lamy's long-running battle with, and replacement of, the Hispanic clergy of New Mexico, Horgan casts Lamy in the light of a benefactor. There are other points of view. For example, Ray John de Aragon says, "Bishop Lamy's removal of the native clergy was tragic. The opinion was formed that New Mexicans were neither educationally nor morally fit for the priesthood. It deprived the Hispanic New Mexicans of their leaders, leaving a 'wound that was long to heal and a scar that can still be felt.' "[47] And Alden Whitman sees Horgan's account of Lamy as "an apologia" in which he identifies much too uncritically with Lamy and the attitudes of the 1840s toward New Mexicans.[48]

Horgan chooses to begin his life of Lamy on 21 May 1839, the date Lamy and Joseph Priest Machebeuf, aged twenty-five and twenty-seven respectively, set off from the village of Riom for Paris and their unknown future. Horgan describes the two friends as fugitives in that Machebeuf's father is unaware of his son's planned trip to America. The scene, with Machebeuf hidden on the floor of the coach as it passes his father's house, has all the narrative force and air of adventure of historical fiction. Horgan's point is that the heritage of the two young priests was with them, "had made them what they were," had given them their past and their character to take into their then unknown future.[49]

Before resuming the narrative of the two friends' escape and the details of their own lives, Horgan spends three brief but important chapters on the history and culture of Auvergne—the home region of the "fugitives." For it is that Romanesque heritage, dating all the way back to Caesar's defeat of King Vercingetorix in the Gallic Wars, that Lamy, in building his cathedral and schools, would transport to Santa Fe. He outlines the Christian humanism that grew in Europe after the Christianizing of Rome by Constantine in 312 A.D. and which, by the twelfth century, penetrated church architecture, French character, and eventually Lamy himself. That humanistic spirit in architecture and religion Lamy carried with him all the way to New Mexico where it is seen today in the Cathedral of St. Francis.

From the sweep across centuries and continents, Horgan zooms in on the city of Clermont-Ferrand, and from there south to the village of Lempdes where Lamy was born in 1814 and the point at which the story of Lamy's life and times begins.

Before Lamy was nine he was enrolled in the Jesuit school at Billom. Later in seminary he met and became friends with Machebeuf. In physical stature and temperament they were unalike: Lamy, tall, dark, and subject to nervous ill-health; Machebeuf, small, pale, and lively. Lamy was nicknamed "the Lamb"; Machebeuf was called "Whitey." As their lives developed, the differences in character remained—"Machebeuf saw with his imagination; Lamy with a sense of recognition" (*L*, 147). Shortly after their ordination they were recruited by the bishop of Cincinnati, John Baptist Purcell, to go to America as missionaries. Machebeuf was destined to become the first bishop of Denver, and Lamy the first bishop and later archbishop of Santa Fe.

From 1839 to 1850 Lamy and Machebeuf worked in the Midwest. For his mission parish Lamy was first assigned to Danville in central Ohio and Machebeuf was given Tiffin close to Lake Erie. The two friends encountered anti-Catholic sentiment and tried to learn English; they had much to do and separated for a time. At Danville, Lamy set about to build his first church, a project that would preoccupy him for much longer and on a much greater scale in Santa Fe. At one point in their Ohio ministry Machebeuf was tempted to go West with the Jesuit missioner P. J. De Smet; when he asked Lamy for advice, the latter replied that he would give up his work in Danville and follow Machebeuf if he went West, little knowing that the tables would one day be turned.

In 1844 Machebeuf's father grew ill and died by the time Machebeuf arrived in France. Sorrowful as that journey was, some resources were gained in that he enlisted the aid of eight nuns and brought them back to America. In 1846 Lamy's father died but the trip to France was postponed until 1848, at which time he persuaded his sister Margaret, a nun, and his young niece, Marie, to return to America with him. (As Sister Francesca, Marie—first as a student in the Loretto Academy and then as a nun in Santa Fe—proved a lifelong comfort to Lamy.) By this time Lamy had been called to serve in Covington, Kentucky; the Mexican War had resulted in new boundaries for the nation through the Treaty of Guadalupe Hidalgo; and the potato famine in Ireland increased Catholic immigration to America and work for the clergy. Nine years had brought much change to Lamy's new country and to him. But the biggest change of all came in 1850. With the expanded boundaries in the Southwest brought about by the Mexican War, a new vicar apostolic was created for the Territory of New Mexico with its see located in Santa Fe. At the age of thirty-five Lamy became the first bishop of New Mexico. Machebeuf agreed to be his vicar general.

Although Lamy's life from 1851 to 1888, from his arrival in New Mexico at thirty-six until his death at seventy-four, provides the major phase of his career and occupies the central portion of Horgan's book, the early years in France and the Midwest are crucial in understanding Lamy's temperament and character. Lamy never wavered in the qualities that won for him election as bishop and later in 1875 the first archbishop of Santa Fe: "Well versed in the doctrine; especially praiseworthy for his mild character, zeal for the salvation of souls, . . . well known for his piety, honesty, prudence, and other virtues" (*L*, 73).

The consecration ceremony which closes the early phase of Lamy's life is one of the most vivid scenes in the entire biography—the result of Horgan's emphathetic witnessing of a real consecration in St. Patrick's Cathedral, positioned behind a curtain with drawing utensils and pad. The imaginative re-creation of Lamy's three-hour consecration is entirely convincing and beautiful in its atmosphere and detail of word, dress, and motion. St. Peter's Cathedral in Cincinnati on 24

November 1850 literally comes to life. It is mildly ironic that Horgan re-creates the entire ceremony in detail but hedges on whether Machebeuf was present. It is, however, a fact of no real consequence in the face of the splendor of the moment.

Lamy and Machebeuf headed for Santa Fe—through that region known on maps of the time as "The Great American Desert"—some two months apart, with Lamy, his sister, and his niece going first. Their route combined river travel down the Ohio and the Mississippi to New Orleans; then by Gulf steamship to Galveston and Indianola in Matagorda Bay; then overland across Texas to San Antonio and El Paso; then the final stretch up the Rio Grande to Santa Fe. Lamy left Cincinnati on 25 November 1850 and arrived in Santa Fe ten months later on 9 August 1851. At New Orleans he left his ailing sister so she could return to France; his niece he left in school. It was an eventful journey filled with hardships which Lamy grew to expect.

Machebeuf caught up with Lamy in San Antonio but under bad conditions. First, Machebeuf brought word that Lamy's sister had died in New Orleans before leaving for France; and, second, Lamy had suffered a severely wrenched leg when jumping from a wagon pulled by mules running out of control. Delayed in their departure again, Lamy used the time to write to Bishop Zubiría in Durango about his appointment, and in studying Spanish with Machebeuf. Finally in May they left San Antonio for El Paso by army wagon train.

Just outside of El Paso Lamy saw the border towns of San Elizario, Socorro, and Isleta—all under the jurisdiction of Bishop Zubiría. It was Lamy's first knowledge of three towns that would cause him decades of bother in attempting to confirm whether Rome wanted Galveston, Durango, or Santa Fe to have charge of them. El Paso and Juarez shocked Lamy, especially at night, with strange customs and wild times, and he feared that Santa Fe might be more difficult than expected. Following the Camino Real north through the river parishes Lamy was well received. Notified of his coming, Bishop Zubiría's rural dean at Santa Fe, Juan Felipe Ortiz, awaited Lamy's arrival. Soon Lamy and Machebeuf came to the conclusion that whatever piety and zeal they saw in the people was superficial and that the fifteen priests for a population of over 70,000 Catholics "were either lacking in zeal or were actually so scandalous in their lives that the state of affairs could not be worse" (*L*, 107).

Realizing that the people could be directed back to a fuller practice of their religion, but wary of a recalcitrant native clergy, Lamy and Machebeuf once in New Mexico passed through another town named Socorro, then Belen, Tomé, Albuquerque, and Bernalillo. Against the silhouette of the Sangre de Cristo Mountains, the bishop and his vicar general entered Santa Fe, welcomed by a large crowd, including the territorial governor and the rural dean, Ortiz. St. Francis church, where Lamy changed into "his purple cassock, surplice, mozzeta, and a heavy white stole embroidered in gold bullion," he found in need of repairs and jarring to his sensibilities. Symbolic of what faced him, Lamy would devote his life to repairing and eventually replacing the church—and reforming what, to his mind and faith, it stood for.

After the ceremony and jubilation of Lamy's entry into Santa Fe, Ortiz, and the local clergy under his leadership, announced to Lamy that they would not accept him as the bishop of their region. Ortiz owed his allegiance to Bishop Zubiría. The rebellion of the native clergy, in refusing to recognize Lamy, would continue for years and would get ugly. The pastor of Taos, Father Antonio Jose Martinez, proved to be a particularly stubborn adversary—as did Albuquerque's pastor, Jose Manuel Gallegos, as much Machebeuf's nemesis as Lamy's. To clarify his authority, in 1851 Lamy traveled on horseback 1,500 miles to Durango and Bishop Zubiría.

Horgan carefully describes the landscape and is lyrical in his account of Lamy's perceptions on this particular adventure. In this southern journey and throughout his accounts of Lamy's numerous trips east across the plains, then west into Arizona, and later, in 1884, again deep into Mexico, Horgan portrays Lamy as a tough plainsman who, like a righteous Josiah Gregg, is as calm and commanding in the face of cholera as he is under Indian attack. Machebeuf was on his little Mexican horse so much that he called himself "El Vicario Andando" ("the Traveling Vicar").

Lamy's 1851 meeting with Zubiría resulted in some vague recognition by Zubiría of Lamy's authority. Zubiría, when presented with Lamy's documents, granted him the validity of his Santa Fe position. The southern New Mexico towns of Doñana, Las Cruces, and Mesilla, and the three border river towns presented issues less easy to resolve. Lamy assumed jurisdiction along the terms of U.S. boundary set by the Treaty of Guadalupe Hidalgo; Zubiría did not, since later map corrections and revised boundary lines did give the lower east-west portion of New Mexico to Chihuahua; thus Zubiría claimed the Las Cruces area. So did Bishop Loza of Sonora. As for the three border towns, they were closest to Durango and, said Zubiría, should be his responsibility. The Gadsden Purchase in 1853 firmly paced Doñana, Las Cruces, and Mesilla in New Mexico and the Vatican accepted them as Lamy's. Lamy, content with Zubiría's sanction of his jurisdiction in Santa Fe, headed back to New Mexico. Zubiría immediately wrote a carefully worded letter to Rome concerning his understanding of his meeting with Lamy. Only after years of trips and correspondence was the matter officially settled.

When Lamy set forth his particulars of reform in a pastoral letter distributed in 1853, Dean Ortiz ordered him out of the rectory, saying it was his house, deeded to him by Zubiría. Ortiz even led a group in public protest against Lamy, Hispanic versus Anglo. Ortiz and Gallegos wrote complaints against Lamy and sent them to Pius IX in Rome. Suspensions of numerous clerics followed: Lujan, Baca, Otero, and Ortiz. Ortiz left for Durango to administer the disputed Doñana towns. Rebellion and resentment were open toward Lamy.

Father Martinez was at first more moderate and compliant toward Lamy, but he continued to speak out on parish divisions and protested the suspensions of his fellows. Martinez sought to retire and asked Lamy to replace him with Father Medina, a local priest and associate. Lamy outmaneuvered him and instead appointed a Spanish priest and again relieved Martinez of all his responsibilities. It was an explosive development. The old priest and his replacement clashed harshly. Schism between Taos and Santa Fe resulted. Martinez was first suspended and as his public accusations against Lamy grew, Machebeuf was sent to Taos to pronounce Martinez excommunicated. Martinez became even more strident in his allegations that all Lamy wanted was money, and that he and Machebeuf were "ravening wolves."

Horgan offers an understanding assessment of the characters of Lamy and Martinez and their quarrel. Horgan finds Martinez miserable in his schism, and portrays him, like Lamy, as a civilizer who attempted, following his own lights, to educate and inform the people of New Mexico, and who, in his "patriotic ire," sought to resist foreign authority of both Anglo-American control and the strict Frenchman, Lamy: "Martinez saw himself as a learned man, a social benefactor, and when made to feel inferior, he was bitterly offended" (*L*, 250). But, Horgan says, Martinez was a victim of "that cultural lag always suffered by a provincial: his ideas had been formed by imported styles of mind long after they had lost novelty at the point of origin" (*L*, 251). Moreover, the two men were of completely different temperament: Martinez an egotist, a master who could not be a servant—Lamy, "self-disciplined in mildness, was a servant in a great domain who knew, when necessary, how to be a master" (*L*, 251).

During Lamy's years of reforming and replacing the native clergy in New Mexico he was busy establishing the means for improving the physical and spiritual well being of his domain. Always the expansionist who worked for bringing the railroad and the world to his remote corner of the country, Lamy, until the arrival of trains in 1880, traveled across the plains by stage coach and wagon.

In 1852, on a long trip East on several matters of business—primarily the first plenary council of bishops in Baltimore, and including stops in New York, Kentucky, New Orleans, and St. Louis—Lamy recruited some Loretto nuns to teach in New Mexico and to colonize the diocese with schools. Lamy's return across the plains with Santa Fe's first nuns resulted in an important friendship with a Santa Fe merchant named Levi Spiegelberg who, though he was suspected of having cholera, Lamy fearlessly took into his party's wagon and nursed back to health. Lamy's supporters—clergy like Purcell in Ohio and Father De Smet in St. Louis, Odin in Galveston, the Society for the Propagation of the Faith in Paris, the Loretto nuns, the grateful Spiegelberg family in Santa Fe, even Kit Carson, Adolph Bandelier, Lew Wallace—all of these allies and others helped make Lamy's accomplishments as a "civilizer" possible.

By the time Lamy became archbishop of Santa Fe in 1875 he could give an impressive accounting of the church's growth in New Mexico under his administration. Even before that, in 1867, Lamy could report to Pius IX on fifteen years of work in the desert. Horgan says of Lamy, "Civilization was emerging under his touch" (*L*, 333). The tally of accomplishments ran as follows: three schools directed by the Christian brothers; schools in all the missions during winter; five schools administered by the Loretto sisters and one by the Sisters of Charity; one seminary underway; six convents of nuns; a hospital and an orphanage opened by the sisters of St. Vincent de Paul.

Lamy died two years after he retired as archbishop in 1885. In his old age he enjoyed sharing the harvests of his own vegetable garden and the seclusion of his home in Tesuque on the outskirts of Santa Fe. There he was visited by young seminarians and others who knew him as an apostle who had worked long in turning the desert diocese of New Mexico into a larger garden with its own human, spiritual, and religious harvests. Lamy's death Horgan describes as "the end of a fine day" (*L*, 440). At seventy-eight he had been a priest for fifty years and a bishop for thirty-eight. Machebeuf followed him in death only a year later. On his triumphant trip to Mexico at the age of seventy-two Horgan says that Lamy "seemed to demonstrate that a great priest was one not less like, but more like, all humanity" (*L*, 423). Separate and together, in their different ways that complemented each other as young men in France and as maturing missioners in America, both Lamy and Machebeuf were indeed great priests.

Horgan's histories of the Rio Grande Southwest, of the lives and times of men like Josiah Gregg and Archbishop Lamy, are similarly great biographies.

Chapter Five

Maker

To understand Horgan's life as Yankee plainsman, writer of fiction, biographer, and historian, is to understand only a part of him as true humanist. His biography in its variety and cosmopolitanism, his transcontinental life pattern, is part of the motives and assumptions of his humanist aesthetic. In this context it is best to regard him, as he does himself, in terms of Stravinsky's reference to the artist as "maker." "My role as a writer," says Horgan, "is to be a maker."[1] Just what goes into making Horgan the maker that he is can best be inferred from his more inspired artistic products. He has, however, written several essays and spoken at length on his humanist aesthetic premises. In his writings, in his work as in his life, one soon comes to realize that his role as maker, his sense of what he calls "analogous form," and of regionalism, are integral parts of his Christian humanism.

Humanist Aesthetic

In 1965 Horgan shared, by way of a brief "felicitation to the Catholic world," his creed as a writer. Point by point, in syllogistic fashion he links questions of beauty with questions of what a writer "ought" to do. His premise is that within the recognition of all life as God's creation all kinds of subjects are free for artistic choice. Christ's being provides evidence of both the ultimate good and the capacity of evil in man's nature. Since man is given the understanding to recognize good and evil and a basis for morality, this conclusion may be reached: "we know that there is no dimension of depth without both light and shadow, so in acts of art there is no revelation of form as the vessel of experience unless we know that moral choice is the very heart of human drama. In this knowledge, the artist, like any man, can find himself in relation to life and work."[2] This perception of the artist viewing both the light and the shadow, good and evil in God's creation and of expressing the conflict and moral choice of man in the form suitable to revealing that "human drama," particularly applies to Horgan's fiction but is evident in his overall persona.

In a 1965 address before the American Philosophical Society, Horgan took issue with what he considered certain inimical and antihumanist influences in society and the abdication of the artist's intuitive sense of the wholeness of man in the face of them. He believes that Marxism, Freudianism, and postcubist styles in literature, art, and music are dangerously partial and fragmented in their views of man. In Horgan's words: "In taking flight toward the abstract, the artist performs a retreat from intuitive all-enclosing humanism and moves toward exclusive intellectual systems in an assumption of a role foreign to his ideal nature and purpose."[3]

Three years later, in further "Reflections on the Act of Writing," he speaks again about the importance of intuition to the true artist-humanist: "The true artist is he who knows without learning. He knows not only with his mind . . . ; he knows with his soul, where flows the fountain of his humanity in its relation to all mankind."[4] He is referring, he says, to man's religious impulse in acknowledging and honoring the creator of all things and awakening the memory of that creation in man through art. Rather than art based on clinical observation and case studies, he prefers art based on "intuitive identity, or loving communion with mankind."[5] In "Toward a Redefinition of Progress," his 1972 address before the Philosophical Society of Texas, he argued—following much the same theme as in "Abdication"—for a new humanism, "looking toward a stable society in which a restored sort of classicism might be found."[6]

Horgan's Christian humanist aesthetic espoused in his essays and addresses also underlies his writings on the practice of individual artists—Randall Davey, Frederick Shrady, N. C., Andrew, and Henriette Wyeth, and Peter Hurd. Always the champion of art that mirrors the human form and image in representational rather than abstract ways, he is a supportive critic of these artists' work. In all of his art criticism runs a correlative assumption about the importance of the artist's biography and his own appreciation of it.

To Horgan, Davey's achievement is a shared vision of "the world made flesh and given elegance."[7] The sculpture of Frederick Shrady's, like his father, Henry Shrady's, pays respect to the dignity of mankind through his treatment of the human figure. If semi-abstract, it is grounded in an understanding of anatomy that "never does violence to the essential truth of natural organic form."[8] Among N. C. Wyeth's many values as painter and illustrator, Horgan is moved by "his love for the beauty of humanity, the face, the form, and the attitude of man and woman."[9] Similarly, Andrew Wyeth eschews the abstract and follows "the ancient desire of the artist to free universal meanings out of those likenesses of life which all men encounter in the same way—the way of seeing *what is there*."[10] In "singing the praises of the obvious," Henriette Wyeth "enters into the company of those master artists . . . whose bequest to the human record retains the essence of life itself" (*HW*, 51).

Horgan has written much about the painting of his friend Peter Hurd: the biographical "portrait sketch," already mentioned; an earlier essay, "The Style of Peter Hurd" (1950); and an essay from remarks made in dedication of the Hurd mural at Texas Technological University on 18 November 1954. Both of the smaller essays are incorporated into the larger "portrait" of Hurd. Horgan praises the mimetic quality of Hurd's art and his allegiance to the "oldest function of art—the representation of life for the purpose of bringing emotional recognition of shared experience."[11] What he likes about Hurd is his resistance to the prevailing nonrepresentational modernist aesthetic. He particularly praises Hurd's murals and goes into considerable analysis of his *South Plains Mural* at Texas Tech. What Horgan says about Hurd as muralist might also be applied to Horgan in that his writings, most notably his Southwestern writings, have a mural-like quality—each work separate and unique but complementing others. This is not to suggest imitation, merely thematic and aesthetic similarity. Horgan identifies the subject of the *South Plains Mural* as Hurd's attempt to show how Lubbock pioneers "brought order out of the wilderness, and human relations out of abstract space" (*PH*, 49). It is the heroic theme on nineteenth-century expansion of America from Atlantic to Pacific in a human lifetime, done in local terms, individual yet representative terms. The presence of this pioneering theme in Horgan becomes more plausible if one sees humanity, each man and woman, facing a new and recurrent frontier in the very act of living. For Horgan as humanist and artist, as Christian "maker," the heart of this "biographical" drama is moral choice—the basis of the realism and "comedy" in his fiction.

Analogous Form

Another part of Horgan's aesthetic is his choice to work in many forms of literature and his supporting belief that music and painting are by analogy helpful to him as an author.

In his acceptance speech upon receiving the Campion Award of the Catholic Book Club in 1957 he explained that the reason he works in many forms is because "a subject for literature creates its own form."[12] He explains that for him any idea for a new work carries with it from the start the architectural terms of its own fulfillment. Out of imagined human circumstances in a given setting comes fiction; out of a real landscape and a sequence of actual happenings comes historical writing; out of emotion perceived as music comes poetry. In Horgan's organic aesthetic, then, form is inherent in content and must be released from within rather than imposed from outside. Nevertheless, he explains that out of such diversity of form in his work one may see a common unifying theoretical objective: "to make a work of literature out of a deep absorption in character and a loving attention to design."[13] By "character" Horgan does not mean only human personality, but something more inclusive which brings vitality to a work. He defines "design" as that which gives a work its appropriate shape. In elaborating on the notion of character, he stresses the importance of human character as his first consideration. In his fiction and biographies he sees character as the lives of people. In his histories, character is people but at times it is place—the Rio Grande or Santa Fe. Design goes much beyond a table of contents into more subtle matters of proportion, rhythm and atmosphere.

Horgan's suppositions about the organic relationship of form and content and the mutual dependency of character and design are not new nor does he claim them to be. He simply expresses this aesthetic with a conviction that it is the human experience which gives meaning and value to artistic process and product. Being an amateur musician and a painter helps him as author. Whereas other art forms do not require an ability to write, he insists that being able to write demands the ability to hear with a musician's ear and see with a painter's eye. For him, "analogous form" is the knack of using the similar processes of music, visual, and written composition. In another essay he extends his theory of analogous form to include the arts of typography and architecture.[14]

Regionalism

As a transcontinental writer and polymath humanist, Horgan's regionalism must be viewed broadly. Insofar as regionalism is a limiting term it does not apply to him. But insofar as regionalism means the embodiment of spirit of place in writing, he is a regionalist in the best sense. He does not regard himself as a regionalist and is puzzled by why so many critics insist on the term: "Everybody is a regionalist. Tolstoy is a regionalist—one is where one lives, where one writes" (H-1). He believes the term came into vogue in the 1920s and 1930s when during depression times the government commissioned many art projects to celebrate various parts of the country and tapped local talent to do so.

In the 1930s Horgan was enthusiastic about the government's stimulation of regionalism in the arts. The Roswell Museum is an instance of help from the WPA Federal Art Program; Horgan found the objectives of that program inherently humanistic and beneficial, and was one of the state advisers for the Federal Art Project of New Mexico. Benefits were many: artists using their talents for the common good; the people understanding that art was for them and not just for high society; the realization that artists were not that different from ordinary citizens; a whole nation turning to art to express its feeling for order. To Horgan the program allowed the local to become a part of man's larger civilization: "We may be proud, then, of how a small city, off by itself on the plains, has managed by enterprise and intelligence to link itself with the great tradition of culture in all other parts of the world; indeed, with all of the good there is in history."[15]

Horgan, from the very beginning of his career in the 1930s when regionalism came into vogue, envisioned a transcendent kind of movement that would bring the local and the universal together in an awareness of a larger humanism of western civilization. His later announcements bear this out. In a symposium on the novel of the American West he says that his education was mainly derived "from the cultural expressions best exemplified in the intellectual and artistic life of the East and of Europe . . . ," and insists that he is not a regionalist, not "a celebrant of any one locale for its own sake."[16] In an even longer statement on "The Pleasures and Perils of Regionalism," he lists one of the perils as self-conscious, stylized, and commercialized regionalism—which he dislikes and avoids because of "the temptation which it carries with it to exploit the *differences* we detect . . . rather than find the universally human and the placelessly significant. . . ."[17] The paradoxical pleasure of regionalism Horgan sees as transcending the limits of the local. Universal man must win out over a specific geography.

In his life and art, in his transcontinental residence and subject matter, and in his aesthetic is variety and, some might say, contradiction. Horgan finds unity in the variety of his life and work:

> The life has had phases but throughout there's been a continuous thread. That's probably a combination of . . . a certain respect for humanism as an attitude and the religious vein . . . and a kind of aesthetic fastidiousness, a sense of choice between the excellent and the good, the beautiful and the adequate. . . . All right, put it down in another very unpopular word: "élite." I subscribe firmly to the value of an élite, provided it has been earned, not bestowed. An élite implies a choice and that I have tried to make, in favor of the superior, the true, and the beautiful. (H-1)

This elitism, explicitly stated here, is implicit throughout his writings. For many who share his humanist values and assumptions about culture, history, and art, that voice resonates favorably. For those of more populist persuasion who see humanist high culture at odds with cultural pluralism, Horgan's voice and tone, his "style," might seem "too civilized." This is a question of reader taste that can only be acknowledged. Unquestionably Horgan is what he is, a "maker," a true artist (*AW*, 90). And his talent as an artist is such that all readers should appreciate what his achievement is rather than what it is not.

Readers

Most critics regard Horgan as an author of Western American literature. There are a few studies, including two dissertations, which consider him as something else than a regionalist. Certainly most newspaper and scholarly reviews point to Horgan's versatility in genre and technique. Reviewers have generally given him good press. Even the few reviewers who find him at times somewhat mannered agree that he is a master prose stylist. Thus much of the best criticism written about Horgan exists in reviews. But the longer evaluations of his work are both perceptive and on the whole sympathetic.

Two important studies of Horgan as a Western writer are James

M. Day's pamphlet, *Paul Horgan* (1967), and William T. Pilkington's *My Blood's Country* (1973). Both of these works are hampered by brevity—Day's because of the pamphlet format, and Pilkington's insofar as only one chapter is devoted to Horgan. Day's scope is more comprehensive than Pilkington's and deals with almost all of Horgan's work up to 1967. Pilkington is concerned with some ten works of fiction up to *A Distant Trumpet* (1960). Both authors are impressed by the extent of Horgan's work and concede that their insights are only partial and premature in that his work would doubtlessly go much beyond the 1960s. Day balances his assessment between both minor and major works and says some significant things only to undercut them by factual mistakes in dates and names. Day concludes that when the final count is in Horgan "will be remembered . . . as an author of fiction rather than history."[18] Pilkington regards Horgan's shorter works like *The Return of the Weed* (read curiously as a novella) as his "most powerful and esthetically complete" and concludes that "it is the author's rounded and true-to-life characters that . . . attract readers to his fiction."[19]

Other studies of Horgan as a Western American writer include Alfred Carter's 1937 essay on the early fiction; Judith Wood Lindenau's assessment of *Mountain Standard Time*; Max Westbrook's introduction to *Far From Cibola*; Jacqueline D. Hall's cassette-lecture on four early novels; and Robert Gish's analysis of *The Common Heart.*[20] Carter's essay is an important initial and prophetic glance at Horgan after the first four novels and places him on a par with Mark Twain for universalizing the regional. Lindenau attempts to explain how Horgan integrates setting with character and theme in his Western trilogy, seeing nature as a primary motivating force in all three novels. Hall in her commentary on *Main Line West, A Lamp on the Plains, The Common Heart*, and *Whitewater*, sees Horgan's persona as substituting the past for original sin and attempting to "exorcise this different devil." As such, his characters are "people whose spiritual alienation is matched by the physical isolation of the plains." Equally provocative in his perceptions, Max Westbrook views *Cibola* as Horgan's "own redaction of ancient myth," a representation of the evil in each human.[21] Gish, in his essay, explicates *The Common Heart* in terms of the interpolated stories within the novel and the way they reinforce the theme of recurrent frontiers in history and humanity.

Broader surveys of Horgan's life and work include the significant essays and provisional bibliography of James Kraft, and dissertations by Stella Cassano Donchak (1970) and Guy LeRoy Cooper (1971). Not that the critical studies which see Horgan in a regional context are in any way meant to reduce Horgan's stature; however, the studies by Kraft, Donchak, and Cooper rightly seek to place him in a wider spectrum of letters.[22] Few critics write as fondly and perceptively about Horgan as does Kraft. In his reading of *Things As They Are* (1964), Kraft places Horgan in the company of James Joyce and anticipates that the "Richard" triptych, when finished, should constitute a true and beautiful fable of American life, "of the nation's growth out of innocence and into maturity."[23] In his 1976 essay on Horgan, Kraft makes of him an American analogue to Henry James, not so much in tensions between Europe and America but in Horgan's juxtaposing of East and West in his life and work. Kraft's cataloging and textual annotating of Horgan's writings to 1973, together with his critical articles, makes him an indispensable Horgan scholar. Likewise, though much more uneven in their perceptions and accuracy of detail, the dissertations thus far on Horgan argue convincingly for recognition of him as more than a minor American author. Donchak confines herself to an analysis of the fiction and tries to illustrate that even though Horgan is not a symbolist writer he is inclined toward allegory. As critic, Donchak is most effective in her reading of Horgan's writings about Abraham Lincoln and in her understanding of female characters—leaving one to wish that the focus of her study had been entirely on Horgan's women. Guy Leroy Cooper writes at great length (and somewhat carelessly) about Horgan and his critical reception. Despite his wide scope he neglects several key works such as *No Quarter Given* and *A Lamp On the Plains*, and mistakenly regards *Men of Arms* as a novel and refers to *A Distant Trumpet* as *A Distant Drum*. Nevertheless, for a roughly chronological reading of Horgan's voluminous work, Cooper succeeds in revealing the real substance which Horgan's mind and art afford.

Mushrooms in the Dark

Few writers are as versatile or as prolific as Horgan. As an author of novels, short stories, histories, biographies, and essays he is a twentieth-century man of letters. His career, which began in earnest in the 1930s, has at present writing continued through five decades and with the 1980s begins a sixth. Never troubled with a lack of things to write about, Horgan has several books underway simultaneously—several short stories which should make another volume as hefty and enjoyable as *The Peach Stone* (1967); and a volume of selected writings is planned by his publisher. Horgan seldom talks about what he is working on or what he intends to write. He simply writes. His books at various stages of preparation seem to grow "like mushrooms in the dark" as he describes it. The fertility of this process is obvious in the books already published, in the short stories in countless magazines, in the essays and lectures and speeches existing in published and unpublished versions. The amount of manuscripts, correspondence, and other related materials in the Horgan collection at the Beinecke Library at Yale fills many boxes.

In this study I have attempted to survey the life and writings of a prolific and versatile American author. What I have asserted here is that Horgan's life and work is a unified though diversified whole. His fiction complements and elucidates his nonfiction. His life story is reflected in the themes, characters, and settings of his novels and histories. His talents as a painter, amateur musician, and writer, are all mutually related and evidenced in his facing life as an artist. They are all expressed as the offerings of a devout Catholic and humanist for the glory of God and man.

Although Horgan is usually classified as strictly a regionalist author he is more accurately seen as a transcontinental writer who infuses in his settings of New York and New Mexico, Texas and California a faith in the best of the European cultural tradition.

The West made a lasting impression on him, the strongest of any region, as a place of freedom, of health, of promise; but for him it is also a place of exile, in need of cultural enlightenment through Anglo-European values and settlement. Horgan's birth in the East, his return to live there and his humanist values confirm his essentially cosmopolitan, "elitist" attitudes toward the cultural wildness and roughness of the West. But in advocating humanist values he seeks not so much to promulgate the differences among cultures and peoples like Native Americans, Hispanics, and Anglo-Americans, as the "common heart of man."

The seemingly "old-fashioned" quality of Horgan's books in the 1980s is due to his essential character and persona as a Christian humanist author writing in the realistic tradition. The act of writing for him is not absurdist gamesmanship. His penchant for moral realism sets him apart from modernist and postmodern novelists. He is his own contemporary in this sense. In another, he is securely placed in the tradition of his twentieth-century literary kin like Willa Cather, Harvey Fergusson, William Goyen, and Wallace Stegner. In some ways, particularly in his emphasis on place, he is not far removed from the greatness of William Faulkner.

Although Horgan has won two Pulitzer Prizes for history and countless honors for his other writing; and although his books have sold hundreds of thousands of copies in many editions, in English and in translation, he remains a relatively neglected author. This is regrettable because as rewarding as Horgan's individual works are, on their own terms, a true appreciation of his achievement depends on a consideration of the magnitude and variety of all his works as a man of letters rather than as either a novelist or a short story writer or a biographer. Admittedly, the body of his work is still incomplete. But what exists is evidence that few American authors in the twentieth century have seen American lives and places so localized and yet so universal.

A "maker" at work in several literary forms and across the continent, Paul Horgan is one of our most inclusive authors. In form and in content his books in all their variety present an amazingly fertile record of American lives and landscapes, a record so abundant that one is compelled to say in admiration of Horgan's achievement, in the words of Thomas Morton's early wonderment at America itself, "If this land be not rich, then is the whole world poore."

Notes and References

Chapter One

1. "Remarks of Paul Horgan, Aspen Award Dinner in Honor of Edmund Wilson, Waldorf Astoria, June 12, 1968," p. 6, manuscript in Horgan archive, Beinecke Library, Yale University.

2. Jacques Maritain, *True Humanism* (New York: Charles Scribner's Sons, 1938), p. xii.

3. *Approaches to Writing*, with a Provisional Bibliography of the Author's Work by James Kraft (New York, 1973), pp. 237–332; hereafter cited as *AW*.

4. See the Report of the Commission on the Humanities, *The Humanities in American Life* (Berkeley: University of California Press, 1980), pp. 1–19.

5. Letter to Gish from Susan Wirth, 8 March 1980.

6. *Peter Hurd: A Portrait Sketch From Life* (Austin, 1965), hereafter cited as *PH*; *Encounters With Stravinsky* (New York, 1972), hereafter cited as *ES*; *Henriette Wyeth* (Philadelphia, 1980), hereafter cited as *HW*. See also, James Kraft, "No Quarter Given: An Essay on Paul Horgan," *Southwestern Historical Quarterly* 80 (July 1976):1–32.

7. Personal interview, Middletown, Connecticut, 6 June 1979. Taped responses by Horgan include: (1) an interview recorded 6 June 1979 in Middletown, Connecticut; (2) a response recorded 23 June 1979; and (3) another recorded 24 September 1980. References to these tapes will be designated H-1, H-2, and H-3 respectively.

8. Afterword to the *The Common Heart*, in *Mountain Standard Time* (New York, 1962), p. 593. Hereafter cited as *MS*.

9. *Buffalo Daily Volksfreund*, 25 February 1922. Beinecke Library, Yale.

10. Susan Wirth is editing the reminiscences of Marie Rohr.

11. "Connecticut Profiles: Paul Horgan," directed by Dennis McGuire (Connecticut Public Television, 5 June 1978).

12. Letter to Gish from Horgan, 24 February 1980.

13. Kraft, "No Quarter Given: An Essay on Paul Horgan," p. 20.

14. Howard Bryan, "Off the Beaten Path," *Albuquerque Tribune*, 10 May 1976, p. A-4.

15. See Susan Dewitt, *Historic Albuquerque Today* (Albuquerque: Historic Landmarks Survey of Albuquerque, 1978), pp. 88–114.

16. "Erna Fergusson and New Mexico: An Introduction," in *New*

Mexico by Erna Fergusson (Albuquerque, 1973), p. x.

17. Interview with T. M. Pearce, Albuquerque, New Mexico, 30 July 1979.

18. *Albuquerque Morning Journal*, 25 June 1922, p. 2.

19. Kyle Crichton, "Contents Noted," *Life*, September 1933, p. 7.

20. "The Old Post," words by Paul Horgan, music by Captain J. B. Darling, Athletic Department, New Mexico Military Institute, ca. 1930.

21. "Bugles in the Sunrise," *New Mexico* 10 (June 1932):10.

22. Horgan to T. M. Pearce, 27 December 1932.

23. Dedicatory remarks of C. Robert McNally, the Horgan Library, 26 November 1970; J. R. Kelly, *A History of New Mexico Military Institute, 1891–1941* (Albuquerque, 1953), pp. 181, 202; "Bulletin on Lt. Col. Paul Horgan, Assistant to the President," n.d. NMMI.

24. Telegram to Colonel J. H. Bearly, 25 November 1970.

25. Horgan, *One of the Quietest Things* (Los Angeles, 1960), hereafter cited as *OQ*; "An Amateur Librarian," *Voices From the Southwest* (Flagstaff, 1976), pp. 65–75.

26. *The Library*, edited by Paul Horgan, assisted by Myron McCormick (Roswell, 1927), p. 4.

27. Kelly, *History*, p. 336. Horgan's teams won the Conference title nine times.

28. Letter to Gish from Hubert Guy, 26 June 1979.

29. Kelly, *History*, p. 354.

30. *The Maverick*, Christmas 1930, p. 5.

31. *Bulletin* (Roswell Museum) 3 (Spring 1955):2.

32. Ibid.

33. Horgan, "The Roswell Museum and Art Center" (Roswell: Roswell Museum and Art Center, 1970), p. 1.

34. Lon Tinkle, *An American Original: J. Frank Dobie* (Boston: Little, Brown and Co., 1978), p. 121.

35. Ibid., p. 116.

36. "About the Southwest: A Panorama of Nueva Granada," *Southwest Review* 59 (Autumn 1974):337–62; originally published summer 1933. See also "The Prairies Revisited: A Re-estimation of Josiah Gregg" 26 (Winter 1941):145–66; "A Tree on the Plains" 28 (Summer 1943): 345–76; "The Cowboy Revisited" 39 (Autumn 1954):285–97; "Mountain to Sea: Rio Grande Notes" 40 (Autumn 1955):325–32.

37. Lawrence Clark Powell, *Great Constellations* (El Paso, 1977), p. 4.

38. Letter to Gish from Dorothy B. Hughes, 24 July 1979.

39. Foreword to *Santa Fe*, by Oliver La Farge (Norman, 1959), p. ix. See also Marta Weigle and Kyle Fiore, *Santa Fe and Taos: The Writer's Era, 1916–1941* (Santa Fe: Ancient City Press, 1982).

40. Letter to Gish from Paul Engle, 11 March 1980.
41. Letter to Gish from Baldwin Maxwell, 6 August 1979.
42. Flannery O'Connor, *The Habit of Being* (New York: Farrar Straus Giroux, 1979), p. 237.
43. *Words for Charles Arthur Henderson*, Memorial Meeting, St. Bartholomew's Chapel, New York, 14 February 1972, p. 5. (Privately published). One hundred copies privately printed for Mary Catherine Cheney Henderson, 1972.
44. Letter from Horgan to Al Mitchell, 18 December 1975.
45. "Connecticut Profiles: Paul Horgan."
46. *The Sense of the Center* (Middletown, Conn.: Wesleyan University, Center for Advanced Studies, 1969), p. 1.
47. "Response . . . to Mark the End of His Service as Director of the Center for Advanced Studies," 4 January 1967, p. 6. Unpublished; Olin Library, Wesleyan University.

Chapter Two

1. John Gardner, *On Moral Fiction* (New York: Basic Books, 1978), pp. 15–16.
2. Gerald Graff, *Literature Against Itself: Literary Ideas in Modern Society* (Chicago: University of Chicago Press, 1979), p. 32.
3. *Humble Powers* (Garden City, N.Y., 1955), p. 8; hereafter cited as *HP*.
4. See "A Note On the Princess Maimonides," *Laughing Horse*, March–July 1928, pp. 8–10.
5. *The Fault of Angels* (New York, 1933), p. 87; hereafter cited as *FA*.
6. E. H. Walton, *New York Times*, 27 August 1933, p. 6.
7. Edward Cornelius, *Saturday Review of Literature* 10 (26 August 1933):61.
8. Clifton Fadiman, *New Yorker* 26 August 1933, p. 54.
9. Alfred Carter, *New Mexico Quarterly* 3 (August 1933):188.
10. James Day, *Paul Horgan* (Austin, 1967), pp. 16–17.
11. Martin Price, *The Oxford Anthology of English Literature* (New York: Oxford University Press, 1973), p. 394.
12. John R. Milton, "The Western Novel—A Symposium," *South Dakota Review* 2 (Autumn 1964):31.
13. Letters from Bynner, 4 and 24 April 1935, Beinecke Library.
14. *Yale Review* 24 (Spring 1935):xi.
15. Mary McCarthy, *Nation* 140 (27 March 1935):367.
16. Seán O'Faoláin, *Spectator* 155 (9 August 1935):236.

17. *No Quarter Given* (New York, 1935), p. 586.

18. *A Lamp on the Plains* (New York, 1937), p. 6; hereafter cited as *LP*.

19. Edith Mirrielees, *Saturday Review of Literature*, 15, 3 April 1937, p. 13.

20. Alfred N. Carter, *Pup Tent*, 27 April 1936, p. 12.

21. Margaret Wallace, *New York Times Book Review*, 14 March 1937, p. 6.

22. Milton, "The Western Novel—A Symposium," p. 31.

23. *Mountain Standard Time*, pp. 277–78.

24. Robert Van Gelder, *New York Times Book Review*, 6 March 1938, p. 7.

25. Otis Ferguson, *New Republic*, 23 March 1938, p. 200.

26. Dorothy Bell Hughes, *New Mexico Quarterly*, 8 May 1938, pp. 130–31.

27. William Du Bois, *New York Times Book Review*, 22 November 1942, p. 40.

28. Stanley Vestal, *Saturday Review*, 2 January 1943, p. 21.

29. Diana Trilling, *New Republic*, 21 December 1942, p. 831.

30. John R. Milton, *The Novel of the American West*, (Lincoln: University of Nebraska Press, 1980), p. 313.

31. *Men of Arms* was intended for young readers and was both written and drawn by Horgan—"for everybody who likes to look at pictures and read about how things are," and is dedicated to ten of Horgan's young friends, including Andrew Wyeth. With profiles in word and picture of twenty-seven soldiers, from "An Egyptian Spearman" to "A War Time Aviator," what Horgan's slim, boldly designed, and long out of print volume attempts is nothing less than the history and evolution of the warrior and the means of warfare—a look at the "many kinds of fighters" (p. 10.)

32. Gaspar Perez De Villagrá, *History of New Mexico* (Los Angeles: Quivira Society, 1933), p. 36.

33. *The Habit of Empire* (New York, 1939), p. 1; hereafter cited as *HE*.

34. *New Republic*, 2 June 1941, p. 769.

35. *A Distant Trumpet* (New York, 1960), p. 1; hereafter cited as *DT*.

36. Frederick H. Guidry, *Christian Science Monitor*, 5 May 1960, p. 9.

37. Paul Engle, *New York Times Book Review*, 17 April 1960, p. 1.

38. Dorothy M. Johnson, *New York Herald Tribune Book Review*, 17 April 1960, p. 1.

39. Mari Sandoz, *Saturday Review* 43 (23 April 1960):51.

40. *Booklist* 56 (1 May 1960):541.

41. *New Yorker*, 23 April 1960, p. 179.
42. *Times Literary Supplement*, 7 October 1960, p. 650.
43. *Middletown Press*, 19 June 1964, p. 1.
44. Judith Crist, *Film Facts* 7 (18 June 1964):104–5.
45. James Day, *Paul Horgan* (Austin, 1967), p. 24.
46. William T. Pilkington, *My Blood's Country* (Fort Worth, 1973), p. 62.
47. Gerald Walker, *Saturday Review* 40 (5 October 1957):17.
48. *Library Journal*, 1 September 1957, p. 2039.
49. Winfield Townley Scott, *New York Herald Book Review* 34 (22 September 1957):4.
50. Arthur Mizener, *New York Times Book Review*, 22 September 1957, p. 4.
51. Peter Buitenhuis, *New York Times Book Review*, 19 June 1966, p. 33.
52. Tom Greene, *America* 114 (21 May 1966):748.
53. Robert B. Dooley, *Catholic World* 204 (October 1966):60.
54. Venetia Pollock, *Punch* 251 (2 November 1966):682.
55. Richard Boeth, *Newsweek*, 12 September 1977, p. 100.
56. *New Yorker*, 12 September 1977, p. 159.
57. Jack Sullivan, *Saturday Review*, 17 September 1977, p. 40.
58. Ivan Gold, *New York Times Book Review*, 11 September 1977, p. 36.
59. James F. Cotter, *America*, 21 September 1968, pp. 220–21.
60. Guy Davenport, *National Review*, 5 November 1968, p. 1120.
61. Alfred C. Ames, *Chicago Tribune Book World*, 8 September 1968, p. 20.
62. Margaret Parton, *Saturday Review*, 8 August 1964, p. 36.
63. Virgilia Peterson, *New York Times Book Review*, 4 August 1964, p. 4.
64. *Newsweek*, 10 August 1964, p. 69.
65. James Kraft, "About Things as They Are," *Canadian Review of American Studies* 2 (1971):48.
66. David L. Minter, *The Interpreted Design as a Structural Principle in American Prose* (New Haven: Yale University Press, 1969), pp. 3–4.
67. *Things As They Are* (New York, 1964), p. 1.
68. *The Thin Mountain Air* (New York, 1977), p. 312.
69. *Everything to Live For* (New York, 1968), p. 215.
70. Max Westbrook, Introduction to *Far From Cibola* (Albuquerque, 1974), p. vii, rightly compares Franz Vosz in *Cibola* to Billy Breedlove in *Whitewater*, noting also that both novels "include the primal act of climbing to a dizzying height."

71. *Whitewater* (New York, 1970), p. 255; hereafter cited as *W*.
72. James Boatwright, *New York Times Book Review*, 27 September 1970, p. 5.
73. Charles Newman, *Nation*, 2 November 1970, pp. 440–41.
74. Denis Donoghue, *New York Review of Books*, 5 November 1970, p. 23.
75. Jamake Highwater, *The Primal Mind* (New York: Harper & Row, 1981), p. 98.
76. *Mexico Bay* (New York, 1982).
77. Jonathan Yardley, "Paul Horgan's Wartime Washington," *Washington Post Book World*, 21 February, p. 3.
78. Johanna Kaplan, "Diana and Admirers," *New York Times Book Review*, 28 March 1982, p. 15.
79. Richard James, "Castles in Sand," *Bloomsbury Review*, December 1982, p. 15.
80. See Robert Gish, "Horgan Reaches Pinnacle," *Chicago Tribune Bookworld*, 14 February 1982, p. 1.

Chapter Three

1. Horgan was encouraged in his early attempts at poetry by Harriet Monroe, Vachel Lindsay, and Witter Bynner. But after a few privately printed poems such as "Villanelle of Evening" (1926), "Lamb of God" (1927), and the poems he published in his own publication, *The Library* (November 1926–May 1927), he soon decided to devote more attention to fiction.
2. Parts of Horgan's novels which appeared in periodicals as shorter fiction include "Slow Curtain" (*Harpers* [1935]), chapter 8 in *No Quarter Given*: "A Try for the Island" (*Harpers* [1942]), part of *The Common Heart*; many chapters from *A Distant Trumpet* which ran in *Collier's* and the *Post*; "First Passion" (*Collier's* [1951]) was included in *Things As They Are* along with "Black Snowflakes" (*Post* [1964]) and "The Spoiled Priest" (*The Critic* [1964]). Several times his short stories have been designated "best of the year" and anthologized. See James Kraft's listing in *Approaches*, 299–314.
3. Pilkington, *My Blood's Country*, p. 51. He asserts that *The Return of the Weed* (1936) is a novel when it is ordinarily read as a collection of short stories.
4. *The Return of the Weed* (New York, 1936), p. 97; hereafter cited as *RW*.
5. See *Peter Hurd: A Portrait Sketch From Life*, pp. 49–56, and chapter 5 of the present study.

6. Eda Lou Walton, *New York Times Book Review*, 22 November 1936, p. 7.
7. Dwight A. Myers, *New Mexico Independent*, 25 April 1980, p. 9.
8. *Figures in a Landscape* (New York, 1940), p. 2; hereafter cited as *FL*.
9. Edith H. Walton, *New York Times Book Review*, 21 April 1940, pp. 6–7.
10. Harry T. Moore, *Saturday Review of Literature*, 8 June 1940, p. 5.
11. *Time*, 29 April 1940, p. 88.
12. *Commonweal*, 4 April 1952, p. 645.
13. Edward J. Fitzgerald, *Saturday Review*, 6 December 1952, p. 37.
14. *New York Herald Tribune Book Review*, 25 December 1955, p. 5.
15. *The Peach Stone* (New York, 1967), p. vi; hereafter cited as *PS*.
16. Flo Wilks, *Albuquerque Journal*, 29 May 1967.
17. Warren Bower, *Saturday Review*, 12 August 1967, p. 30.
18. Frederick Jackson Turner, "The Significance of the Frontier in American History," in *The Frontier Thesis*, ed. Ray Allen Billington (New York: Holt, Rinehart and Winston, 1966), p. 9.
19. "The Fortress, 1772," "Taos Valley," *Yale Review*, September 1944, p. 40. "The Isleta Priest," "Episodes from the Passionate Land," in *Folk-Say: A Regional Miscellany* (Norman, 1929), pp. 120–21.
20. Pilkington, *My Blood's Country*, p. 61.
21. Day, *Paul Horgan*, p. 10.
22. *The Saintmaker's Christmas Eve* (New York, 1955), pp. 10–11.
23. *The Devil in the Desert*, in *The Peach Stone*, pp. 406–38.
24. Pilkington, *My Blood's Country*, p. 61.

Chapter Four

1. Ralph Waldo Emerson, "History," in *Complete Writings* (New York: William H. Wise & Co., 1929), p. 127.
2. *Great River: The Rio Grande in North American History* (New York, 1954), pp. xiii-xviii, hereafter cited as *GR*; *The Heroic Triad: Essays in the Social Energies of Three Southwestern Cultures* (New York, 1970), pp. vii–ix.
3. *Yale Review* 23 (September 1933):212.
4. "Erna Fergusson and New Mexico: An Introduction," in *New Mexico: A Pageant of Three Peoples*, p. xii.
5. Maurice Garland Fulton and Paul Horgan, eds., *New Mexico's Own Chronicle* (Dallas, 1937), pp. x–xi.
6. "Survey Southwest," in *Look at America: The Southwest* (Boston,

1947), pp. 9–34; "New Mexico," *Saturday Evening Post*, 27 January 1962, pp. 15–21.

7. In *Rome Eternal* (New York, 1959), Horgan says, "Rome is the spiritual center of the world, for you . . ." (p. 146).

8. *From The Royal City of The Holy Faith of St. Francis of Assisi*, (Santa Fe, 1936); *Centuries of Santa Fe* (New York, 1956).

9. Walter Prescott Webb, *Saturday Review*, 8 December 1956, p. 22.

10. Oliver La Farge, *New York Times Book Review*, 7 October 1956, p. 4.

11. Bernard Kalb, *Saturday Review*, 16 October 1954, p. 13.

12. D. W. Brogan, *Times Literary Supplement*, 22 July 1955, p. 408.

13. Milton S. Byam, *Library Journal*, 1 September 1954, p. 1498.

14. *Time*, 1 November 1954, p. 102.

15. Oliver LaFarge, *New York Herald Tribune*, 10 October 1954, p. 1.

16. J. Frank Dobie, *New York Times Book Review*, 10 October 1954, p. 1.

17. Walter Prescott Webb, *Saturday Review*, 16 October 1954, p. 13.

18. Stanley Walker, *New Yorker*, 4 December 1954, p. 230.

19. Frank D. Reeve, "A Letter to Clio," *New Mexico Historical Review* 31 (April 1956):132.

20. La Farge, *New York Herald Tribune*, 10 October 1954, p. 13; see also *New York Times Book Review*, 7 October 1956, p. 4.

21. Dobie, *New York Times Book Review*, 10 October 1954, pp. 1, 41.

22. Webb, *Saturday Review*, 16 October 1954, p. 13.

23. Fergusson to Horgan, 5 October 1955, Beinecke Library, Yale. Also see Catherine C. Mundell, "Paul Horgan and the Indians: *Great River* as a Historical Failure," unpublished M.A. thesis, The University of Texas at El Paso, 1971.

24. Edel to Gish, 9 September 1979.

25. Edel to Horgan, 23 November 1970, Beinecke Library, Yale.

26. See *Telling Lives*, ed. Marc Pachter (Washington: New Republic, 1979).

27. "George Washington," in *The American Historical Scene* (New York, 1936), p. 13.

28. Paul Engle, *New York Times Book Review*, 23 April 1961, p. 22.

29. *Citizen of New Salem* (New York, 1961), p. 93.

30. Vincent Price to Gish, 18 June 1980.

31. *Death, Mr. President* (Roswell, 1937–39, 1942).

32. *Songs After Lincoln* (New York, 1965), p. 69.

33. DeWitt Bell, *New York Times Book Review*, 7 November 1965, p. 72.

34. W. T. Scott, *Saturday Review*, 9 October 1965, p. 58.

35. *Josiah Gregg and His Vision of the Early West* (New York, 1979); hereafter cited as *JG*.

36. Joseph A. Cawley, S. J., *Best Sellers*, November 1979, p. 296.

37. Alden Whitman, *Books & Arts*, 26 October 1979, p. 14.

38. William McDonald, *Lone Star Book Review*, November 1979, p. 15.

39. "In Search of the Archbishop," *Catholic Historical Review* 46 (January 1961): 409–27; "Convergences Toward a Biography," *Wesleyan Library Notes* 5 (Autumn 1970):1–8.

40. "Preface to an Unwritten Book," *Yale Review* 65 (March 1976): 324–26. See also Robert Gish, "Paul Horgan and The Biography of Place," *Prairie Schooner* 55 (Spring–Summer '82):226–32.

41. Willa Cather, *On Writing* (New York: Alfred A. Knopf, 1949), p. 12.

42. Will Hoffman, *Albuquerque Journal*, 10 August 1975, p. D–2.

43. Dennis Halac, *Commonweal*, 26 March 1976, p. 211.

44. Mayo Mohs, *Time*, 10 November 1975, p. 95.

45. F. D. Reeve, *Yale Review* 65 (Winter 1976): 289–92.

46. Edmund Fuller, *New Mexican*, 10 August 1975, p. 20.

47. Ray John de Aragon, *Padre Martinez and Bishop Lamy* (Las Vegas: Pan-American Publishing Co., 1978), p. 115. See also Fray Angelico Chavez, *But Time and Chance: The Story of Padre Martínez of Taos, 1793–1867* (Santa Fe: The Sunstone Press, 1981).

48. Alden Whitman, *Albuquerque Tribune*, 13 May 1976, p. B–6.

49. *Lamy of Santa Fe* (New York, 1975), p. 4; hereafter cited as *L*.

Chapter Five

1. Hugh Gallagher, "Paul Horgan, Author," *Albuquerque Journal*, 14 August 1977, p. D–1.

2. "A Writer's Creed," *Catholic World* 201 (April 1965):15.

3. "The Abdication of the Artist," *American Philosophical Society* 109 (October 1965):270.

4. "Reflections on the Act of Writing," *Wesleyan Quarterly* 5 (Winter 1968):5.

5. Ibid.

6. "Toward a Redefinition of Progress," *Proceedings of the Philosophical Society of Texas* 35 (1973):15.

7. Preface to *Randall Davey* (New York, 1967), p. 2.

8. "The Sculpture of Frederick Shrady," *Critic*, April–May 1967, p. 62.

9. Foreword to *N. C. Wyeth* (New York, 1972), p. 11.

10. "Andrew Wyeth," *Ramparts* 2 (Christmas 1963):71.

11. "The Style of Peter Hurd," *New Mexico Quarterly* 20 (Winter 1950–51):421.

12. "Character and Form in Creative Writing," *America*, 25 May 1957, p. 260.

13. Ibid., p. 261.

14. "The Serene Severities of Typography" (Middletown, Conn., 1966).

15. "Roswell Museum," *Roswell Daily Record*, 3 October 1938, p. 4.

16. John R. Milton, "The Western Novel—A Symposium," *South Dakota Review* 2 (Autumn 1964):27–28.

17. "The Pleasures and Perils of Regionalism," *Western American Literature* 8 (Winter 1974):169.

18. Day, *Paul Horgan*, p. 38.

19. Pilkington, *My Blood's Country*, pp. 51, 63.

20. Alfred Carter, "On the Fiction of Paul Horgan," *New Mexico Quarterly* 7 (August 1937):207–16; Judith Wood Lindenau, "Paul Horgan's *Mountain Standard Time*," *South Dakota Review* 1 (May 1964): 57–64; Max Westbrook, Introduction to *Far From Cibola* (Albuquerque, 1974), pp. v–xiii; Jacqueline D. Hall, "The Works of Paul Horgan" (Deland, Fla., 1976); Robert Gish, "Albuquerque as Recurrent Frontier in . . . *The Common Heart*," *New Mexico Humanities Review* 3 (Summer 1980):23–33.

21. Westbrook, Introduction, p. ix.

22. James Kraft, "About Things As They Are," *Canadian Review of American Studies* 2, no. 1 (Spring 1971):48–52; "No Quarter Given: An Essay on Paul Horgan," *Southwest Historical Quarterly* 80, no. 1 (July 1976):1–32; and Bibliography to *Approaches to Writing* (New York, 1973), pp. 237–332; Stella Cassano Donchak, "Paul Horgan: Craftsman and Literary Artist" (Ph.D. diss., Case Western Reserve University, 1970); Guy Leroy Cooper, "Paul Horgan: American Synthesis" (Ph.D. diss., University of Arkansas, 1971).

23. Kraft, "About *Things As They Are*," p. 48.

Selected Bibliography

PRIMARY SOURCES

1. Novels

A Distant Trumpet. New York: Farrar, Straus and Cudahy, 1960; New York: Paperback Library, 1971.

A Lamp on the Plains. New York: Harper & Brothers, 1937.

The Common Heart. New York: Harper & Brothers, 1942.

Everything to Live For. New York: Farrar, Straus and Giroux, 1968; New York: Popular Library, 1968.

Far from Cibola. New York: Harper & Brothers, 1938; Albuquerque: University of New Mexico Press, 1974.

The Fault of Angels. New York: Harper & Brothers, 1933.

Give Me Possession. New York: Farrar, Straus and Cudahy, 1957; New York: Paperback Library, 1971.

The Habit of Empire. Santa Fe: Rydal Press, 1939.

Main Line West. New York: Harper & Brothers, 1936.

Memories of the Future. New York: Farrar, Straus and Giroux, 1966; New York: Ballentine Books, 1968.

Mexico Bay. New York: Farrar, Straus and Giroux, 1982.

Mountain Standard Time. New York: Farrar, Straus and Cudahy, 1962; New York: Popular Library, 1966.

No Quarter Given. New York: Harper & Brothers, 1935.

The Thin Mountain Air. New York: Farrar, Straus and Giroux, 1977.

Things As They Are. New York: Farrar, Straus, 1964; New York: Paperback Library, 1971.

Whitewater. New York: Farrar, Straus and Giroux, 1970; New York: Paperback Library, 1971.

2. Short Fiction

"The Burden of Summer." *Folk-Say IV*, edited by B. A. Botkin. Norman: University of Oklahoma Press, 1932, pp. 134–47.

The Devil in the Desert. New York: Longmans, Green, 1952.

"Episodes from the Passionate Land." *Folk-Say: A Regional Miscellany*, edited by B. A. Botkin. Norman: University of Oklahoma Press, 1929, pp. 120–24.

Figures in a Landscape. New York: Harper & Brothers, 1940.

"Figures In a Landscape." *Folk-Say: A Regional Miscellany*, edited by

B. A. Botkin. Norman: University of Oklahoma Press, 1931, pp. 185–94.
Humble Powers. London: Macmillan, 1954. Garden City, N.Y.: Image Books, 1955.
One Red Rose for Christmas. New York: Longmans, Green, 1952.
The Peach Stone. New York: Farrar, Straus and Giroux, 1967; New York: Paperback Library, 1971.
The Return of the Weed. New York: Harper & Brothers, 1936; Flagstaff: Northland Press, 1980.
The Saintmaker's Christmas Eve. New York: Farrar, Straus and Cudahy, 1955; Santa Fe: William Gannon, 1978.
"Taos Valley." *Yale Review* 34, no. 1 (September 1944):36–56.

3. Histories, Biographies, and Other NonFiction
"A Writer's Creed." *Catholic World* 201, no. 1 (April 1965):15.
"The Abdication of the Artist." *Proceedings of the American Philosophical Society* 109, no. 5 (October 1965):267–71.
"About the Southwest: A Panorama of Nueva Granada." *Southwest Review* 59, no. 4 (Autumn 1974):337–62.
"An Amateur Librarian." In *Voices From the Southwest*. Flagstaff: Northland Press, 1976, pp. 65–75.
Approaches to Writing. New York: Farrar, Straus and Giroux, 1973; New York: Noonday Press, 1974.
"Bugles in the Sunrise." *New Mexico* 10, no. 6 (June 1932):10–12, 47–48.
The Centuries of Santa Fe. New York: E. P. Dutton & Co., 1956; Santa Fe: William Gannon, 1976.
"Character and Form in Creative Writing." *America*, 25 May 1957, pp. 260–62.
"Churchman of the Desert." *Horizon* 7, no. 6 (October 1957):30–35, 99–101.
Citizen of New Salem. New York: Farrar, Straus and Cudahy, 1961; New York: Avon Books, 1968.
Conquistadors in North American History. New York: Farrar, Straus and Co., 1963.
"Convergences Toward A Biography." *Wesleyan Library Notes*, no. 5 (Autumn 1970), pp. 1–8.
"Critical Essay." In *Selected Poems of Witter Bynner*, edited by Robert Hunt. New York: Alfred A. Knopf, 1936, pp. xxiii–lxix. In the 1943 edition, pp. 263–309.
Encounters With Stravinsky. New York: Farrar, Straus and Giroux, 1972.
"Erna Fergusson and New Mexico." In *New Mexico: A Pageant of Three*

Peoples, by Erna Fergusson. Albuquerque: University of New Mexico Press, 1973, pp. ix–xx.

Foreword to *N. C. Wyeth*, by Douglas Allen and Douglas Allen, Jr. New York: Crown Publishers, 1972, pp. 11–13.

Foreword to *Santa Fe*, by Oliver La Farge. Norman: University of Oklahoma Press, 1959, pp. v–x.

From the Royal City. Santa Fe: Rydal Press, 1936.

Great River. New York: Holt, Rinehart and Winston, 1954; New York: Minerva Press, 1968.

Henriette Wyeth. Chadds Ford: Brandywine Conservancy, 1980.

The Heroic Triad. New York: Holt, Rinehart and Winston, 1970; New York: World Publishing, 1971.

"Indian Arts." *Yale Review* 22, no. 1 (September 1932):205–8.

"In Search of the Archbishop." *Catholic Historical Review* 46, no. 4 (January 1961):409–27.

Josiah Gregg and His Vision of the Early West. New York: Farrar, Straus and Giroux, 1979.

"Journey to the Past—and Return." *Texas Quarterly* 13, no. 2 (Summer 1970):34–51.

Lamy of Santa Fe. New York: Farrar, Straus and Giroux, 1975; New York: Farrar, Straus, and Giroux, 1980.

Maurice Baring Restored. New York: Farrar, Straus and Giroux, 1970.

"New Mexico." *Saturday Evening Post* 235, no. 4 (27 January 1962): 15–21.

"New Mexico." *Yale Review* 23, no. 1 (September 1933):211–13.

New Mexico's Own Chronicle. Dallas: Banks Upshaw and Company, 1937. Coeditor Maurice Garland Fulton.

One of the Quietest Things. Los Angeles: University of California School of Library Science, 1960.

Peter Hurd: A Portrait Sketch From Life. Austin: University of Texas Press, 1965.

"The Pleasures and Perils of Regionalism." *Western American Literature* 8, no. 4 (Winter 1974):167–71.

Preface to *Randall Davey*. New York: Findlay Galleries, 1967, pp. 2–3.

"Preface to an Unwritten Book." *Yale Review* 65, no. 3 (March 1976): 321–35.

"Reflections on the Act of Writing." *Reflection: The Wesleyan Quarterly*, no. 5 (Winter 1968), pp. 2–6.

Rome Eternal. New York: Farrar, Straus and Cudahy, 1959.

"The Sculpture of Frederick Shrady." *Critic*, April–May 1967, pp. 59–65.

"The Serene Severities of Typography." Middletown, Conn.: Wesleyan University, Art Laboratory, 1966.

"The Spirit of the Fiesta." *Yale Review* 24, no. 3 (March 1935):630–32.

"The Style of Peter Hurd." *New Mexico Quarterly* 22, no. 4 (Winter 1950–51):420–26.

"Survey Southwest." In *Look at America: The Southwest.* Boston: Houghton Mifflin, 1947, pp. 9–34.

"Toward A Redefinition of Progress." *Philosophical Society of Texas* 35 (1973):8–18.

4. Poetry

"The Mask." *Poetry* 26, no. 4 (July 1925):205–7.

Songs After Lincoln. New York: Farrar, Straus and Giroux, 1965.

"Westward." *Poetry* 43, no. 3 (December 1933):144–49.

"Why and Wherefore of Billy the Kid." *Maverick*, Christmas 1930, p. 5.

5. Drama, Juvenile, Miscellaneous

"A Tree On the Plains: Libretto of the Opera." *Southwest Review* 28 (Summer 1943):345–76.

"Death, Mr. President." Roswell, June 1937–July 1939, 1942. Unpublished; Beinecke Library, Yale.

The Library, nos. 1–7. Roswell: New Mexico Military Institute, 1927.

Men of Arms. Philadelphia: David McKay Company Publishers, 1931.

Toby and the Nighttime. New York: Farrar, Straus and Co., 1963.

SECONDARY SOURCES

1. Bibliographies

Kraft, James. "A Provisional Bibliography." In *Approaches to Writing*, by Paul Horgan. New York: Farrar, Straus and Giroux, 1973, pp. 237–322.

2. Books and Articles

Carter, Alfred. "On the Fiction of Paul Horgan." *New Mexico Quarterly* 7 (August 1937):207–16. Considers the first four published novels.

Day, James. *Paul Horgan.* Austin: Steck-Vaughn, 1967. First study of Horgan as Southwestern author. Some factual mistakes.

"Festschrift for Paul Horgan." Edited by Tom Corcoran and Jon Appleby. Aspen: Aspen Institute for Humanistic Studies, 1973. Tributes by Robert Giroux, Virginia Rice, and others.

Gish, Robert. "Albuquerque as Recurrent Frontier in . . . *The Common Heart.*" *New Mexico Humanities Review* 3, no. 1 (Summer 1980): 23–33. Analyzes interpolated histories in the novel.

Kelly, J. R. *A History of New Mexico Military Institute, 1891–1941.*

Albuquerque: University of New Mexico Press, 1953. Specifics of Horgan's years at NMMI.

Kraft, James. "About *Things As They Are*." *The Canadian Review of American Studies* 2, no. 1 (Spring 1971):48–52. Anticipates completion of the Richard trilogy.

———. "No Quarter Given: An Essay on Paul Horgan." *Southwestern Historical Quarterly* 80, no. 1 (July 1976):1–32. Consideration of Horgan's biography.

Lindenau, Judith Wood. "Paul Horgan's *Mountain Standard Time*." *South Dakota Review* 2, no. 1 (Autumn 1964):27–32. Sees trilogy as reflecting American restlessness.

Milton, John R. "Paul Horgan." *South Dakota Review* 2, no. 1 (Autumn 1964):27–32. Major statement by Horgan on Western writers.

Pilkington, William T. "Paul Horgan." In *My Blood's Country: Studies in Southwestern Literature*. Fort Worth: Texas Christian University, 1973, pp. 51–64. Comprehensive view of Horgan's fiction to 1960.

Powell, Lawrence Clark. *Great Constellations*. El Paso: El Paso Library Association, 1977. Praise for Horgan and Hurd as regionalists.

Reeve, Frank D. "A Letter to Clio." *New Mexico Historical Review* 31, no. 2 (April 1956):102–32. Indictment of *Great River* as history.

3. Video Tapes and Cassettes

"Connecticut Profiles: Paul Horgan." Connecticut Public Television, 5 June 1978. Alexander Scourby interviews Horgan at home in Middletown, Connecticut.

Hall, Jacqueline D. "The Works of Paul Horgan." Western American Writers Cassette Curriculum. Deland, Fla.: Everett/Edwards, 1976. Lecture on *Main Line West, A Lamp on the Plains, The Common Heart*, and *Whitewater*.

4. Dissertations

Cooper, Guy Leroy. "Paul Horgan: American Synthesis." Ph.D. dissertation, University of Arkansas, 1971. Survey of Horgan's early, middle, and late career as writer.

Donchak, Stella Cassano. "Paul Horgan: Craftsman and Literary Artist." Ph.D. dissertation, Case Western Reserve University, 1970. Assigns Horgan a modest place as an American novelist.

Index